# Supervision in Psychoanalysis

This book originates from a series of clinical supervisions that were held by Antonino Ferro at the São Paulo Institute of Psychoanalysis. *Supervision in Psychoanalysis: The São Paulo Seminars* reproduces in their entirety the dialogues in the seminars that followed these supervisions.

The transcripts of eight supervised clinical sessions, along with the author's comments, allow the reader to:

- see the different styles of the presenting analysts first-hand;
- understand the evaluation of Bion's thinking, as developed by the author.

With detailed exposure of clinical sessions, their supervision and clarification of the theoretical model of the supervisor, this book will be of interest to psychologists, psychotherapists and psychoanalysts.

**Antonino Ferro** is President of the Italian Psychoanalytic Society and also Consultant Associate Editor of the *International Journal of Psychoanalysis*. He is a training and supervising analyst in the Italian Psychoanalytic Society, the American Psychoanalytic Association and the International Psychoanalytical Association. He has been a visiting professor of psychoanalysis in various institutions in Europe, North America, South America and Australia. He received the Sigourney Award in 2007.

THE NEW LIBRARY OF PSYCHOANALYSIS
General Editor: Alessandra Lemma

The New Library of Psychoanalysis was launched in 1987 in association with the Institute of Psychoanalysis, London. It took over from the International Psychoanalytical Library which published many of the early translations of the works of Freud and the writings of most of the leading British and Continental psychoanalysts.

The purpose of the New Library of Psychoanalysis is to facilitate a greater and more widespread appreciation of psychoanalysis and to provide a forum for increasing mutual understanding between psychoanalysts and those working in other disciplines such as the social sciences, medicine, philosophy, history, linguistics, literature and the arts. It aims to represent different trends both in British psychoanalysis and in psychoanalysis generally. The New Library of Psychoanalysis is well placed to make available to the English-speaking world psychoanalytic writings from other European countries and to increase the interchange of ideas between British and American psychoanalysts. Through the *Teaching Series*, the New Library of Psychoanalysis now also publishes books that provide comprehensive, yet accessible, overviews of selected subject areas aimed at those studying psychoanalysis and related fields such as the social sciences, philosophy, literature and the arts.

The Institute, together with the British Psychoanalytical Society, runs a low-fee psychoanalytic clinic, organizes lectures and scientific events concerned with psychoanalysis and publishes the *International Journal of Psychoanalysis*. It runs a training course in psychoanalysis which leads to membership of the International Psychoanalytical Association – the body which preserves internationally agreed standards of training, of professional entry, and of professional ethics and practice for psychoanalysis as initiated and developed by Sigmund Freud. Distinguished members of the Institute have included Michael Balint, Wilfred Bion, Ronald Fairbairn, Anna Freud, Ernest Jones, Melanie Klein, John Rickman and Donald Winnicott.

Previous general editors have included David Tuckett, who played a very active role in the establishment of the New Library. He was followed as general editor by Elizabeth Bott Spillius, who was in turn followed by Susan Budd and then by Dana Birksted-Breen.

ALSO IN THIS SERIES

*Impasse and Interpretation* Herbert Rosenfeld
*Psychoanalysis and Discourse* Patrick Mahony
*The Suppressed Madness of Sane Men* Marion Milner
*The Riddle of Freud* Estelle Roith
*Thinking, Feeling, and Being* Ignacio Matte Blanco
*The Theatre of the Dream* Salomon Resnik
*Melanie Klein Today: Volume 1, Mainly Theory* Edited by Elizabeth Bott Spillius
*Melanie Klein Today: Volume 2, Mainly Practice* Edited by Elizabeth Bott Spillius
*Psychic Equilibrium and Psychic Change: Selected Papers of Betty Joseph* Edited by Michael Feldman and Elizabeth Bott Spillius
*About Children and Children-No-Longer: Collected Papers 1942–80* Paula Heimann. Edited by Margret Tonnesmann
*The Freud–Klein Controversies 1941–45* Edited by Pearl King and Riccardo Steiner
*Dream, Phantasy and Art* Hanna Segal
*Psychic Experience and Problems of Technique* Harold Stewart
*Clinical Lectures on Klein & Bion* Edited by Robin Anderson
*From Fetus to Child* Alessandra Piontelli
*A Psychoanalytic Theory of Infantile Experience: Conceptual and Clinical Reflections* E Gaddini. Edited by Adam Limentani
*The Dream Discourse Today* Edited and introduced by Sara Flanders
*The Gender Conundrum: Contemporary Psychoanalytic Perspectives on Femininity and Masculinity* Edited and introduced by Dana Breen
*Psychic Retreats* John Steiner
*The Taming of Solitude: Separation Anxiety in Psychoanalysis* Jean-Michel Quinodoz
*Unconscious Logic: An Introduction to Matte-Blanco's Bi-logic and its Uses* Eric Rayner
*Understanding Mental Objects* Meir Perlow
*Life, Sex and Death: Selected Writings of William Gillespie* Edited and introduced by Michael Sinason
*What Do Psychoanalysts Want?: The Problem of Aims in Psychoanalytic Therapy* Joseph Sandler and Anna Ursula Dreher
*Michael Balint: Object Relations, Pure and Applied* Harold Stewart
*Hope: A Shield in the Economy of Borderline States* Anna Potamianou
*Psychoanalysis, Literature & War: Papers 1972–1995* Hanna Segal
*Emotional Vertigo: Between Anxiety and Pleasure* Danielle Quinodoz
*Early Freud and Late Freud* Ilse Grubrich-Simitis
*A History of Child Psychoanalysis* Claudine and Pierre Geissmann

*Belief and Imagination: Explorations in Psychoanalysis* Ronald Britton
*A Mind of One's Own: A Psychoanalytic View of Self and Object* Robert A Caper
*Psychoanalytic Understanding of Violence and Suicide* Edited by Rosine Jozef Perelberg
*On Bearing Unbearable States of Mind* Ruth Riesenberg-Malcolm
*Psychoanalysis on the Move: The Work of Joseph Sandler* Edited by Peter Fonagy, Arnold M. Cooper and Robert S. Wallerstein
*The Dead Mother: The Work of André Green* Edited by Gregorio Kohon
*The Fabric of Affect in the Psychoanalytic Discourse* André Green
*The Bi-Personal Field: Experiences of Child Analysis* Antonino Ferro
*The Dove that Returns, the Dove that Vanishes: Paradox and Creativity in Psychoanalysis* Michael Parsons
*Ordinary People, Extra-ordinary Protections: A Post Kleinian Approach to the Treatment of Primitive Mental States* Judith Mitrani
*The Violence of Interpretation: From Pictogram to Statement* Piera Aulagnier
*The Importance of Fathers: A Psychoanalytic Re-Evaluation* Judith Trowell and Alicia Etchegoyen
*Dreams That Turn Over a Page: Paradoxical Dreams in Psychoanalysis* Jean-Michel Quinodoz
*The Couch and the Silver Screen: Psychoanalytic Reflections on European Cinema* Andrea Sabbadini
*In Pursuit of Psychic Change: The Betty Joseph Workshop* Edited by Edith Hargreaves and Arturo Varchevker
*The Quiet Revolution in American Psychoanalysis: Selected Papers of Arnold M. Cooper* Arnold M. Cooper, Edited and Introduced by Elizabeth L. Auchincloss
*Seeds of Illness and Seeds of Recovery: The genesis of suffering and the role of psychoanalysis* Antonino Ferro
*The Work of Psychic Figurability: Mental States Without Representation* César Botella and Sára Botella
*Key Ideas for a Contemporary Psychoanalysis: Misrecognition and Recognition of the Unconscious* André Green
*The Telescoping of Generations: Listening to the Narcissistic Links Between Generations* Haydée Faimberg
*Glacial Times: A Journey through the World of Madness* Salomon Resnik
*This Art of Psychoanalysis: Dreaming Undreamt Dreams and Interrupted Cries* Thomas H. Ogden
*Psychoanalysis and Religion in the 21st Century: Competitors or Collaborators?* David M. Black
*Recovery of the Lost Good Object* Eric Brenman
*The Many Voices of Psychoanalysis* Roger Kennedy

*Feeling the Words: Neuropsychoanalytic Understanding of Memory and the Unconscious* Mauro Mancia
*Constructions and the Analytic Field: History, Scenes and Destiny* Domenico Chianese
*Projected Shadows: Psychoanalytic Reflections on the Representation of Loss in European Cinema* Edited by Andrea Sabbadini
*Encounters with Melanie Klein: Selected Papers of Elizabeth Spillius* Elizabeth Spillius
*Yesterday, Today and Tomorrow* Hanna Segal
*Psychoanalysis Comparable and Incomparable: The Evolution of a Method to Describe and Compare Psychoanalytic Approaches* David Tuckett, Roberto Basile, Dana Birksted-Breen, Tomas Böhm, Paul Denis, Antonino Ferro, Helmut Hinz, Arne Jemstedt, Paola Mariotti and Johan Schubert
*Time, Space and Phantasy* Rosine Jozef Perelberg
*Rediscovering Psychoanalysis: Thinking and Dreaming, Learning and Forgetting* Thomas H. Ogden
*Mind Works: Techniques and Creativity in Psychoanalysis* Antonino Ferro
*Doubt Conviction and the Analytic Process: Selected Papers of Michael Feldman* Michael Feldman
*Melanie Klein in Berlin: Her First Psychoanalyses of Children* Claudia Frank
*The Psychotic Wavelength: A Psychoanalytic Perspective for Psychiatry* Richard Lucas
*Betweenity: A Discussion of the Concept of Borderline* Judy Gammelgaard
*The Intimate Room: Theory and Technique of the Analytic Field* Giuseppe Civitarese
*Bion Today* Edited by Chris Mawson
*Secret Passages: The Theory and Technique of Interpsychic Relations* Stefano Bolognini
*Intersubjective Processes and the Unconscious: An Integration of Freudian, Kleinian and Bionian Perspectives* Lawrence J. Brown
*Seeing and Being Seen: Emerging from a Psychic Retreat* John Steiner
*Avoiding Emotions, Living Emotions* Antonio Ferro
*Projective Identification: The Fate of a Concept* Edited by Elizabeth Spillius and Edna O'Shaughnessy
*Creative Readings: Essays on Seminal Analytic Works* Thomas Ogden
*The Maternal Lineage* Edited by Paola Mariotti
*Donald Winnicott Today* Edited by Jan Abram
*Symbiosis and Ambiguity: A Psychoanalytic Study* Edited by John Churcher, José Bleger and Leopoldo Bleger
*Psychotic Temptation* Liliane Abensour
*Supervision in Psychoanalysis: The São Paulo Seminars* Antonino Ferro
*Transference and Countertransference Today* Robert Oelsner

## TITLES IN THE NEW LIBRARY OF PSYCHOANALYSIS TEACHING SERIES

*Reading Freud: A Chronological Exploration of Freud's Writings* Jean-Michel Quinodoz
*Listening to Hanna Segal: Her Contribution to Psychoanalysis* Jean-Michel Quinodoz
*Reading French Psychoanalysis* Edited by Dana Birksted-Breen, Sara Flanders and Alain Gibeault
*Reading Winnicott* Lesley Caldwell and Angela Joyce
*Initiating Psychoanalysis: Perspectives* Bernard Reith, Sven Lagerlöf, Penelope Crick, Mette Møller and Elisabeth Skale
*Infant Observation* Frances Salo
*Reading Anna Freud* Nick Midgley

## TITLES IN THE NEW LIBRARY OF PSYCHOANALYSIS 'BEYOND THE COUCH' SERIES

*Under the Skin: A Psychoanalytic Study of Body Modification* Alessandra Lemma
*Engaging with Climate Change: Psychoanalytic and Interdisciplinary Perspectives* Edited by Sally Weintrobe
*Research on the Couch: Single Case Studies, Subjectivity, and Psychoanalytic Knowledge* R.D. Hinshelwood
*Psychoanalysis in the Technoculture Era* Edited by Alessandra Lemma and Luigi Caparrotta

# Supervision in Psychoanalysis

## The São Paulo Seminars

Antonino Ferro
Translated by Ian Harvey

Routledge
Taylor & Francis Group
LONDON AND NEW YORK

First published 2013
by Routledge
27 Church Road, Hove, East Sussex BN3 2FA

Simultaneously published in the USA and Canada
by Routledge
711 Third Avenue, New York, NY 10017

*Routledge is an imprint of the Taylor & Francis Group, an informa business*



*British Library Cataloguing in Publication Data*
A catalogue record for this book is available from the British Library

*Library of Congress Cataloging in Publication Data*
Ferro, Antonino, 1947-
Supervision in psychoanalysis : the Sao Paulo seminars / Antonino Ferro.
pages cm. -- (The new library of psychoanalysis)
Includes bibliographical references and index.
1. Psychoanalysis--Study and teaching. I. Title.
RC502.F47 2013
616.89'170076--dc23
2012047853

ISBN: 978-0-415-58754-9 (hbk)
ISBN: 978-0-415-58755-6 (pbk)
ISBN: 978-0-203-38005-5 (ebk)

Typeset in Bembo
by Saxon Graphics Ltd, Derby

# Contents

# Foreword by Maria Olympia de A. F. França

This book is essentially clinical in nature. The creative spirit of Antonino Ferro is present in every moment of his work; his generosity in transmitting his ideas is enormous. In these seminars, commenting on the ideas expounded by our colleagues in São Paulo, he allows us to get to know his conception of his analytical work in an extremely vivacious way. He thus becomes an author who, in a similar way to Freud, tries to engage his interlocutors in a lively exchange.

The Kleinian conception of projective identification caused a great transformation and expansion in our way of understanding the analytic space. The idea of interdependence between subject and object became fundamental to the analytic understanding of the creation and development of subjectivity. Subsequently, Bion was able to pinpoint, with greater clinical and theoretical subtlety, the function of communicating projective identification. It is in this context that contributions by authors such as Ferro have their place; writers who know how to "see" the apparatus for thinking in its element, and the $\alpha$ function at the point when it is still in a nascent state in the encounter between the two parties of the analytic couple.

Ferro invites us to approach patients with the aim of encountering them in the dream through which they will be revealed. We have been able to share this language thanks to the heritage left to us by Bion, and especially thanks to our masters. These masters have made use of the dream as an expression of the humanistic and aesthetic vertex of psychoanalysis, capturing in the emotion the essential content of the encounter, humanizing it and embodying it in images and words.

The exchange of ideas presented in this book demonstrates clearly that Brazilian psychoanalysis is definitely part of the context of modern and current epistemological thinking.

In reproducing the dialogues from these seminars we have tried to be as faithful as possible to the original text, and we hope that we have been able to stimulate in the reader the spirit of curiosity and reflection that involved all of us present.

# Acknowledgements

**Analysts in supervision:**

Alícia Beatriz D. Lisondo, Ana Maria S. Vannucchi, Edoara Paron Radvany, José Otávio Fagundes, Luciana Gentilezza, Maria Cecília P. da Silva, Maria Lucía Ferrão de Souza Campos, Maria Tereza De Barros França, Miriam Malzyner, Vera Regina Fonseca.

I would like to thank Antonino Ferro for authorizing this publication. We would also like to mention the invaluable cooperation of those colleagues who were generous and courageous enough to allow the use of their clinical material for this study.

As Scientific Director of the Brazilian Psychoanalytical Society of São Paulo, during the period 1995–1996, I was able to rely on the limitless collaboration of the then-president Leopold Nosek in organizing these seminars, and also that of Luiz C. Ulhôa Junqueira, President of the Brazilian Psychoanalytical Society of São Paulo, on the occasion of these seminars, as well as Evelise S. Marra, João Baptista N. F. França, Magaly Thomé, Maria Cecilia P. da Silva, Nilde P. Franch and Sandra Gonçalves.

My thanks go to Lidia Aratangy for her excellent work in revising the texts, and to Maria Celina Anhaia Mello for her participation in organizing this book.

I am grateful to Ana Maria Vannucchi, Edáorada Radvany, Lucina Gentilessa and Marta Petricciani for their excellent simultaneous translation during the clinical seminars. Thanks to the competence, love and enthusiasm she dedicated to the work, Marta Petricciani's contribution to the organization of this book has been invaluable.

To all our patients, who are the sources of inspiration for the ideas presented in this book, goes our respect and our gratitude.

Maria Olympia de A. F. França

# Introduction

These seminars are the faithful reproduction of supervisions I held at the Brazilian Psychoanalytical Society in São Paulo, Brazil, in November 1996. Together with Anne Alvarez, Elizabeth and Mercello Bianchedi, Parthenope Bion, Robert Caper, Florence Guignard and Otto Kernberg, I was in São Paulo to attend a congress about Bion's ideas, organized by the Brazilian Psychoanalytical Society. On that occasion, I was asked to come before the congress, in order to hold the seminars contained in this book over a period of three days. I had no previous knowledge of the material or the themes, so it really was a case of live "cooking". Four seminars took place on Monday, 11 November, 1996: three on the Tuesday; and the last three on the Wednesday.

This invitation came soon after the translation into Portuguese of my book *The Bi-Personal Field: Experiences in Child Analysis*, which had provoked some comment.

I am still grateful to Elias Mallet Da Rocha Barros, who "discovered" my book, to Maria Olympia de A. F. França, at the time Scientific Secretary of the Brazilian Psychoanalytical Society in São Paulo, and to the Presidents L. Nosek and L. C. Ulhôa Junqueira. My gratitude also goes to the translators, who had the difficult task of translating on the spot and, in particular, to Marta Petricciani, who was responsible for the translation of my books published in Brazil.

I found these seminars very rewarding, both on a scientific and cultural level (there was already a basic affinity thanks to our common passion for Bion's ideas), and on the human and personal level, because of the generosity and warmth of the Brazilian colleagues.

In this brief introduction, I would like to add some points that have "matured" in my practice of supervision and which represent — in terms of frequency — the most common factors in my work. I shall explain these concepts briefly:

- With some patients I think it is necessary to limit oneself to grasping the emotion present in the communication, emphasizing it and thus making it something shared and manifest, before going on to make interpretations of content.
- I think it is equally necessary to grasp the quality of the response to the interpretation. Each interpretation causes turbulence, and the effects of this turbulence are usually visible in the first communication after this interpretation. I say "usually" because the "response" to the interpretation does not necessarily occur immediately, or with linear causality.
- It is necessary to modulate the subsequent interpretive event while bearing in mind the patient's "response"; this can range from a minimal intervention up to a maximal event, from an unsaturated, narrative interpretation to an interpretation saturated with transference and content.
- Grasping the "response" to the interpretation does not, therefore, necessarily mean not interpreting it (and thus modifying the interpretative structure), nor necessarily interpreting it: the oscillation between these two extremes constitutes the *art* of psychoanalysis.
- In many cases the negative characters ("the man with the stick", "the witch", "the violent man" etc.) that one may be tempted to interpret immediately as parts or functions of the patient, should, when possible, be "worn" by the analyst for a long time as modes in which the patient sees him. Otherwise, they must be left with the "characters" where they have been placed.
- The way the patient sees us (say, "the man with the stick") can, at times, be interpreted as "sometimes I am afraid that I might be ready to hit you violently", or, in an implicit way: "it is terrible to feel threatened by someone at your back". The choice between the two modes belongs — once again — to the *art* of psychoanalysis, with its various layers of experience and sensitivity in listening to the patient's replies.
- There are emotions that can be interpreted directly from the patient straightaway. First of all, anger, disappointment, being

hurt, then later, jealousy or fragility. However, more time is necessary for violence, aggressiveness, sadism and envy. Envy is often self-interpreted by the patient as soon as they have a "place to keep it". This general statement must, however, be qualified on an ad hoc basis. The point is that the patient cannot immediately have the space necessary for parts that are difficult to integrate — otherwise, why would they have split them off? — and more time and work is necessary to develop this potential in the patient (in Bion's terms this means fostering the development of the patient's alpha function, and their function as a "container").

- The session and every mental state within it *also* have to do with what is going on in the analytic relationship in the present. There are splits in time (past and future) and splits in space (characters), which *also* refer unequivocally to emotional events in the consulting room. Splits and cleavages are not necessarily to be interpreted, but can be "played out" as one would in child analysis.
- How should we propose changes in the setting? This is one of the moments that mark the asymmetry between analyst and patient more than any other. They should be requested with a certain amount of advance warning. There must be something the patient is already aware of in the initial contract; let's say, "periodically the fee will go up". Since it signals asymmetry, it will be greeted by the patient with anger and pain: "I had a dream," said the patient, "where I lost sight of my daughter. I found her again with her dress dirty, perhaps bleeding, like in the Sophia Loren film *La Ciocara* (*Two Women*) … it was like it was a painful growth, but a growth … it's like being in the hospital where I went from being a student to considering myself as someone who works there …". It is this being a victim of violence, but also this unavoidable rite of passage, which makes possible a leap in their mental life, and a realization of their status as patient that also brings with it an acceptance of the state of asymmetry. What is "hit" is the "agglutinated nucleus" (Bleger) that has various layers in the setting, and which thus emerges and gives rise to metabolization.
- After a transference interpretation, a young female patient jumps up and says, by way of reply: "I have been stung by an insect, here's the swelling". The interpretation is a major source of turbulence and an $\alpha$ element — a proto-visual thought element — has formed. As we know, it is initially unknowable: it is an emotional pictogram that is like a Polaroid photo still facing

inwards. But we can know its *narrative derivative*: "I was bitten by an insect, here's the swelling" is a narrative derivative that describes a pictogram which has given form, colour and expression to an experience of surprise, pain and irritation. Other equally meaningful narrative derivatives could have been chosen. "When I was small, my father often hit me, and it left a mark"; or "On TV I saw a lorry that demolished a row of cars because the driver ignored the stop sign"; or "At nursery school, my little brother was thrown to the ground by a terrible boy in his class, and he started to bleed"; or "I remember an episode of *ER* in which they had to re-animate some people who had been hurt by robbers and there was a lot of blood" ... and so on, in an infinite number of other narrative derivatives of the same α element.

- The character often needs to be respected: "My grandmother's cat is desperate because my grandmother is away. How can I explain to the cat that my grandmother is away but will come back? The thing is I can't take it to my house because I have a leather sofa that would get ruined". The patient's need not to see his skin lacerated by the split-off part must be respected. This communication was made by a teenager just before Christmas.
- Interpretations: with some patients it is essential to intervene centrifugally, from the centre to the periphery, in such a way that the field expands and takes on meaning. With other patients, it is necessary to move in the opposite direction, focusing on the centre and moving from the edge to the centre of the present relationship. Different patients also mean the same patient at different moments in their analysis, or at different moments of the same session. Every patient at every session ought to be regarded as an unknown patient and every session a "first session". This is the meaning of "without memory and desire".
- Pronoun friends: some pronouns such as *others*, *someone*, and so on, are like comfortable "oven gloves" that enable us to take hold of emotions that are still too hot to handle, or which are given in a direct and explicit form. "It is always painful to be separated from someone one likes" could already be more of a transference interpretation for a patient who says that she doesn't like not being able to see her boyfriend over the Christmas holidays. Or to another patient, who talks of the fear of being abandoned, one could say: "It is terrible to feel abandoned by someone you need".

- Another important concept is what I call the "semantic nest", which is a kind of niche in the discourse, where highly significant emotional truths, camouflaged by language, find a nest, but in such a chameleon state that they are also said as a means of "escaping". At some point in the session, a female patient talks a lot about "entropy", chaos and so on. The analyst gets lost in this apparently boring topic, without understanding the "nest" that is there. The patient describes how she "entro/pia" and then finds herself in chaos. That is to say, she is talking about how she *enters piously (pia)*, quietly, tranquilly into the session, and then feels disorientated by interpretive activity by the analyst that exceeds her capacity to tolerate it. Another patient, after having denied any emotional involvement in their analysis, talks about the intense and moving experience of reading about "Little's analysis with Winnicott". Another nest: in their adult part the patient is really not very interested in the analysis, because what they bring to the analysis is "little", the infantile part of themself, which is very involved in the analysis.
- It may often be useful to understand the functions the field can take on in a particular place, by describing the traits of the "characters".
- In some analyses the contemporaneous administration of drugs may be necessary. What is important is that the "external drug" begins to enter the session at some point. Stefano has started taking Entumin, and at some point he dreams that some players have entered the world of football but are losing games, and there is a referee who failed to see when players were offside. Without any prompting he says that taking Entumin is something that makes him feel calm, but now he is too calm. This represents him taking his place in the analysis but losing opportunities to do analytic work, with a referee who does not communicate the breaks in the setting. At this point, I can tell him that inside the session there is also a kind of Entumin that can make him feel too calm, in a non-constructive way, and that this Entumin seems, in my opinion, to have taken the form of his sitting face-to-face so as to have more control over the situation; thus he is watching me and not lying down. This Entumin also consists of the tests he submits me to, asking me "if he will get better" — a question that demands a reply — and other occasional breaks in the setting (asking to go to the toilet, phone calls from his mother), even

though these things were necessary for a long time to make the analysis tolerable to him. Now we can start to think not only of reducing further his real intake of Entumin, but also what he takes in these ways during the session. He replies: "a dream told me that the tests are not even very useful, psychoanalysis is better, and another that it is right to see where the platelets are produced inside the marrow". In this way, he becomes aware that Entumin, breaching the setting, makes this work more difficult. And in another dream he signals: "a coach has to do many manoeuvres" to find the right road. It is also clear, however, that for a long time Entumin (in all senses) had been necessary.

- Some interpretations are regarded as unacceptable by the patient for a long time because they are a source of distress ("my colleague who is always touching me up really annoys me"; "I found a pornographic magazine in my pigeon hole at school and I know who must have left it", in reply to interpretations). But at some point, the patient makes these interpretations easily and quite normally, on their own. Romina talks about dreaming of two parents who lose two children, and about mines that blow two legs off someone; then a girl on the stairway of the analysis burdened with a sense of guilt, who makes love with a particularly sexy colleague, and then goes on to comment on — I would say, to *interpret* — her dreams on her own. I say that the two lost children and the two legs blown off make her think of two missed sessions because of the double holiday; the girl in lingerie suggests the subject of sexuality broached at the last sessions, which was now present, even though she still felt ashamed; and making love with the sexy friend was like the ability to re-appropriate an aspect of herself she had always feared and denied. Of course, the analyst must be a presence that fosters insights and transformations.

Antonino Ferro

# Thematic Seminar I

COORDINATOR: The purpose of this evening's thematic seminar — on the subject of the analyst's dream — is to help us learn something about Antonino Ferro's theoretical concepts. Clinical material will form the starting point for some reflections and comments by Dr Ferro, after which we will have the opportunity to exchange ideas. In tune with Dr Ferro's ideas, we shall work in an unsaturated manner, without knowing in advance what will come out.

ANALYST IN SUPERVISION: Luís, a fifty-year-old manager, has been in analysis for a little over four years. He comes three times a week. He has already done two other analyses that lasted several years. The session described here took place after an absence of two weeks. His work involves a lot of travelling, which forces him to miss sessions quite frequently, but he has never been away for such a long time.

*Luís enters, says hello, puts his coat on the chair, lies down and says immediately, with a sarcastic tone:*

PATIENT: I haven't been for a long time. *(Silence)* You must be angry with me.

ANALYST: Maybe it's you who's angry with me and that's why you haven't been.

PATIENT: Analysis is very difficult for a man who works as hard as I do. I've had meetings and been on business trips. How could I have been here? I couldn't have stopped travelling or told the others to wait because I had to go to my analysis. *(Silence)*

*During the silence I feel the tension in our meeting again. I feel something stormy in the air, a sense of hostility. I think that he is talking in order to show me the importance of his work, and to demonstrate how tiring it is being with me and with his inner world. It feels as if something is about to collapse and I am afraid I won't be able to hold it up.*

*Luís resumes, this time in an irritated tone.*

PATIENT: Besides, the analysis is useless. It hasn't changed my problem with women. I just repeat things.

ANALYST: I'm amazed that you keep coming and paying for something that is so useless. I think that you are struggling in this analysis to make me harmless and to paralyse me. Or might it be because you want to paralyse your need for contact?

PATIENT *(after a pause)*: What I wanted to do was to paralyse time, life, my age. I don't want to grow old. I don't want to retire. This seems to me like the end. I think I'll always feel useless and without any importance. The passing of time is so horrific! I also don't want time to pass for S. *(his secretary and lover)*. I don't want her to get old either. She used to be so beautiful and now she, too, is getting old. I can see the signs of it more and more, even though she is still thin. I ought to find myself a younger lover, but I can't. My marriage with M. has been over for some time. I never accepted her and I kept on putting her to the test all the time. I think I'm putting you to the test here as well. I'm examining you. I think I still haven't accepted you as my analyst, just like I've never accepted my wife. How can I accept you if I've never seen your CV and don't even know if you're a doctor? My previous analyst was a doctor and a professor. I came here because you were recommended by A., a former patient of yours.

*Luís had talked about being attracted to A. on several previous occasions, but he was intimidated by her as she was a beautiful and intelligent artist.*

ANALYST: You test me and you denigrate me, to make me feel what you feel when you denigrate your women and yourself.

*(Long silence)*

PATIENT: I've been watching that insect on the window. The insect can't fly *(I think it was a fly or a wasp)*. It's trapped because the pane of glass is in the way and it's not looking for a way out, which would be right there next to it … That's the way I feel. I'm imprisoned by these three women *(the wife, the lover-secretary and the work colleague)*, a fourth, who is a young woman from New York, and a fifth who is even younger; another work colleague. *(Ironic tone)* Do you know who Don Giovanni is?

*(I keep silent)*

PATIENT: I feel like Don Giovanni, who tries to have women but is unable to enjoy them.

*I imagine a desired and potent Don Giovanni parading his various women. I imagine a frail insect, alone and imprisoned. I see an unusual, tragic-comic scene: Luís as an insect dressed up as Don Giovanni. Perhaps he creates hitches in the analysis so as not to lose his costume and to avoid collapse.*

*I say:*

ANALYST: You test your potency with women, and with me you test my knowledge to find out if I can cope with your fear of fragility, loneliness and destruction.

*(Silence)*

PATIENT: I don't know why, but just now I remembered a dream I had last night (*the patient hasn't recounted dreams during the session for some time*). I don't know if it's worth talking about it, because I don't see any connection with anything. Obviously you're going to say that it's something coming from my unconscious, but I can't see anything in it.

ANALYST: You want to know everything, and you don't want to have to rely on me.

PATIENT: I dreamt about the boarding school I attended for eight years. I was very unhappy there. In the dream, I visited the school and found all the doors to the classrooms closed. I also saw the room where I took the school entrance exam. On the patio I saw seven swimming pools overflowing with water. The priests didn't feature in the dream. Then I saw some schoolmates from that time, but they were the age they are now.

ANALYST: What do you think about the dream?

PATIENT: I was thinking about how the priests had made a lot of money with the school. There used to be only one swimming pool.

ANALYST: You seem to see the priests as exploiters. When you are afraid that I am exploiting you here as well, and that I'm not interested in you as a person, you feel unhappy and you don't get anything out of the analysis.

PATIENT *(emphatically)*: But I have got something out of the analysis. I can get on with people better at work and also with my children. *(Silence)* Ah! Now I remember that at my school there was a kind of punishment we used to call "arrest". Do you know what "arrest" involved?

ANALYST: No.

PATIENT: It's when a pupil did three things wrong and was then suspended. I was afraid of it, and was always anxious not to get "arrested".

*At that moment I imagined a robot stuck to the window pane, hanging by its legs and smashed to pieces.*

ANALYST: I think you are anxious you might be suspended and totally destroy your contact with other human beings. Here in the analysis you are putting me to the test to see if I can take it and to see whether I'm going to suspend our contract as well.

PATIENT: But I was away on business. *(Pause)* Yes, I think I am putting you to the test to see if you will suspend me or not.

*The session ends.*

DR FERRO: I would like to begin with the clinical material, although I am not exactly sure how to start. The material is good; it's rich and interesting, and it lends itself to various possible interventions.

I would like to look again at the session a piece at a time, and to let things flow gradually, bearing in mind above all the analyst's dream, and the way in which the characters inside the session can be understood.

The first character to take shape in the analysis — which is announced even before the session itself — is the patient's work. I would see the patient's work as the first character in the session, in the sense that work is something he does in the outside world, which prevents him from coming to the session. However, we can also see it as inner work; the work the patient performs on himself. But what I would like to focus on is the type of work the patient does inside the analytic situation. And this applies to all the characters in the session. If a patient talks about the cat he used to have, it might mean that he is talking about his cat and his feelings towards his cat, or that he is talking about the cat as an internal object, which may (or may not) be projected on to the analyst. We might also think that he is talking about something feline in the relationship.

There is a wonderful lithograph by Escher, with the title *Relativity*, in which various floors are joined by various stairways, and it is not clear in which direction these stairs go, or how they join up. The characters can be seen as standing on various stairways and in various ways. On one stairway the character is a real figure; on another the character is the patient's internal object; on yet another — in my view, the most significant — the character is something that is connected specifically to what is happening inside the session. I shall focus my attention above all on this third type.

I have the impression that the patient's work inside the session, or inside the analysis, consists in stopping time. He performs his job by not coming to the session. This is his "work"; he has to stop time. Perhaps you remember the Bergman film, *Wild Strawberries*. It opens with the dramatic scene of a funeral and a clock with no hands. I think that this patient's work consists of constantly removing the hands from the clock; he is a busy man — engaged primarily in avoiding thinking, like a hyperactive child who has to keep running this way and that, so as not to fall into a deep abyss of despair. At some point, the patient says this, when he talks about paralysing time, life, his age. This reminds me of the tale by Edgar Allen Poe, *The Purloined Letter*, where the best way of hiding something is to make it very obvious.

It seems to me that the psychic truth of this patient lies in this refrain: "I want to paralyse time, life, my age". But his way of making sure that this is not discovered is precisely to put it on display, to exhibit it as something of no importance, so that the analyst sets about looking elsewhere. The patient keeps on saying: "I don't want to get old. I don't want to retire". Even retirement can be thought of as a character in the analysis: retirement as the end of his work, and also as the end of his analysis. To put it another way: "I have to stay with you because there is a drama that cannot be faced alone; the drama of passing time, things that finish".

Then he goes on to talk about S, the secretary-lover, who is also getting old. One can think of her as S. and also as the analysis, since time passes also for the analysis, and it changes from month to month. Luís can see it on his own face and on the face of the analyst, and it's tragic. It's as if there is a problem, such as that which might occur in a midlife crisis, which generally speaking is transient and tolerable.

I thought of the depressive movement we find at the beginning of Dante's *Divine Comedy* — "In the middle of the journey of our life I came to myself within a dark wood where the straight way was lost" — which is a way of representing the impact of middle age. The advantage is that, in the past, this happened to people at the age of thirty, whereas nowadays it comes much later. Elliot Jacques makes the point that the only way one can work through and overcome midlife crisis is through creativity. I am not referring specifically to midlife crisis, but to all the existential crises we pass through: adolescence, middle age, reaching the age of sixty, and the crisis of senility.

I like what the patient says at some point about the analyst having been recommended, by A. We can see A. as the real person who recommended the analyst but also, on the stairway that interests me most, we could think of A. as the creative capacity of the patient. But he is intimidated, frightened at this prospect. He finds it easier to carry on with his job of stopping time. We could start a kind of dream about this material that has rich echoes in a number of literary figures: *The Picture of Dorian Gray*, Fellini's *Casanova* etc.

Then the analyst registers the patient's process of demeaning himself, and tries to get progressively closer to him — and here we have the image of the insect as something which, in some way, carries away and represents movement. It is interesting because the analyst gives the interpretation of Luís's disparaging attitude towards women *after* the patient has spoken of A.; in other words, after the patient has spoken of his potentially creative part. For me, this is the analyst's first dream. It is as if he dreamt of having to give this interpretation about the patient's contempt for women immediately after speaking about A. When the patient feels that the analyst is coming closer to the part we are calling A., something living comes out: the movement of the insect. But the glass pane is in the way, preventing the insect from flying. The patient says he feels imprisoned by three women, and then a fourth comes on the scene, and a fifth. It is almost like a way of pointing to his feeling of being imprisoned by three analyses, and perhaps by a fourth and a fifth.

At some point, the patient investigates: "Do you know who Don Giovanni is?". Here, the hidden things that are laid out in plain sight on the table are picked up from the discussion about Don Giovanni. Here, we have a reverie on the part of the analyst, in which he imagines an insect dressed up as Don Giovanni. At this moment there is a situation of impasse, embodied in the figure of the insect: an insect that is by no means inoffensive, but whose sting could, in fact, cause a fatal illness because it is the insect that speaks of time, of the end of things and of death. In order to remain hidden, it must be covered up with clothes, like Don Giovanni or Casanova.

I think the analyst is very close to the patient when he asks if he can face up to fragility, loneliness and destructiveness — which are basically represented by death — and the patient replies with a dream, almost as if, at this moment, he feels able to enter into contact with something profound, something with which the analyst can, in his turn, make contact.

I would now like to hear the associations you have with this dream, because I feel I can't have very many fantasies in this context; it is almost as if there were too many closed doors.

I think the doors refer to the impossibility of the idea of sharing at this moment. The seven swimming pools brim-full of water refer, I am not quite sure why, to a mythical and biblical theme. I associate them with the Bergman film *The Seventh Seal*, and the scene with the terrible chess game between the Knight and Death, where Death inevitably takes all the Knight's pieces.

Another intense moment is when the analyst picks up the patient's drama: his feeling of being alone and, at the same time, not being able to take advantage of the analysis. This is the other drama: not being able to use A., but always having to stop time instead of transforming his anguish into something creative. The analyst picks up this drama and the patient replies by saying that he has achieved something — he has improved in his work and in his relations with his family — as if, at that moment, a small door had opened to let in A.

To conclude: when he talks about the robot stuck to the window pane, suspended by its legs, this is another insight by the analyst. I think this robot represents the actual functioning of the patient, which is mechanical — exactly the opposite of what A. does, who is an artist. The patient, on the other hand, tries to stop time in an automatic way, and to prevent any movement in the analysis. The central dream seems to me the analyst's dream about this insect that must not be allowed to sting the pair. One could see this from a classical point of view as an impasse in which there is an area of resistance on the part of the pair, inside which there is a place that cannot be metabolized. However, I prefer to see it as something the analyst and patient are working on.

AUDIENCE: I imagine, Dr Ferro, that you are in some way referring to the idea of the Barangers, namely the *bulwark* or the *bastion*, which is a point of resistance.

DR FERRO: Yes, we'll come back to that during our discussion. It is as if there were a creative function in the work of the analytic pair, A., who circulates at moments of contact between analyst and patient, and who could melt the iceberg that stands in the way of thought.

Many years ago, I wrote a paper on countertransference dreams. It is clear that today we mean something different; that is to say, we bracket out countertransference dreams, the activity the analyst engages in outside the session. Rather we think of what Bion calls waking "dream thought", which is the basic function the analyst develops when he has a reverie. In other words, when he enters into contact with his own mental image. However, the formation of the analyst's α function is something ongoing, and the analyst's interpretations offer the patient the narrative derivatives of these α elements. The analyst does not know the α elements that are forming at every moment, prompted by the patient's stimuli. Or, to put it another way, the α elements as such are not knowable by the analyst, even though, at every instant, he continues to form α elements based on his own stimuli. The analyst enters into contact with the α elements when he has a reverie; that is, when he enters into contact with a visual image, since the α element is the emotional pictogram of that instant of the relationship. In this instant of reverie, he is in contact with the waking dream function of his mind.

The same happens to the patient. He continues to dream the session in real time, and all he knows of his dream are the narrative derivatives of the α element. In other words, when the analyst gives the interpretation, this acts as a stimulus to the patient to form the α element, and he creates an emotional photogram of how he has experienced the analyst's interpretation. Generally, he cannot know this α element in itself, but he makes a narrative derivative out of it; that is, he finds real-life characters and situations which bear some kind of relationship with the α element that has formed. The exception, however, is in the very special situation — somewhat similar to that of the analyst's reverie — of waking dream photograms. These are not hallucinations but elusive α elements which are seen by the patient from the outside, so not as a fantasy of seeing something. The analyst has a reverie and says: "I have had a fantasy of an insect dressed up as Don Giovanni". But in the patient's waking dream photogram there is a pictogram that is elusive, but is also seen.

I have many patients, especially borderline patients, where this dream function of the mind is very evident; it is neither hallucination nor dream, but something that happens in the waking state. The first time I observed the illustrative and even comic capacity of the α element was once when I informed a patient about a fee increase. Her response was to say: "My God, on the wall over there I can see a chicken being feathered". I also recall a child who wanted to stop the analysis. I was not convinced this was the right thing to do; it was a very serious case and the child had had hallucinations in the past, real hallucinations. I tried to put off finishing the analysis and he had a visual flash: "I can see a pair of pliers pinching me".

The α element is also produced continually during the session by the patient, and only awaits being narrated, because, apart from situations where the analyst has a reverie or the patient has a visual flash, we know nothing about this α element except for its derivatives, which of course are necessarily distorted.

Analyst in supervision: When you spoke of the danger of the insect, I remembered a joke a patient once told me. A scorpion wants to cross a river and asks a frog to carry it over to the other side. The frog says: "I'm afraid you'll sting me". The scorpion replies: "I won't sting you, because if I did, we'd both die during the crossing". Then, as they are crossing the river, the scorpion stings the frog, who says: "But you said you weren't going to sting me! Now we're both going to die!". And the scorpion replies: "Yes, but there's nothing I can do about it. It's in my nature ...".

AUDIENCE: I was thrilled by the words of Dr Ferro, because what I've heard today coincides with an idea I have developed in my work over the last twelve years, something I called "intuitive images". This idea of the analyst's spontaneous mental images has been developed extensively under the name of reverie, only that instead of putting the emphasis on the α function, which is of course present, I emphasize the process of communication that becomes established in the analytic couple.

The process of communication corresponds to the description of what Bion called "reverie"; in other words, normal projective identification. By means of the normal process of projective identification, the patient communicates to the analyst important intuitions which are deposited in the analyst and he, in possession of this communication, has a spontaneous image of great creative power. At this point, the analyst has to interpret the meaning of the image that has been deposited inside him. So, he has the image itself and the interpretation, or the meaning of the image, which he can transmit to the patient. At the moment when he decodes the image and gives it a psychoanalytic meaning, he can guide the process, not only in terms of the oneiric significance of the session, but also with regard to the meaning of what is happening. I am struck by the fact that I find echoes of work I am developing in what Dr Ferro says.

AUDIENCE: Although, on the one hand, the potency and vitality the analyst shows towards this analysand is highly valuable, on the other hand, these qualities come across as an affront to someone who presents himself as a kind of Egyptian Pharaoh. The Seven Plagues came to mind. With reference to the character you call A., what would be the fantasies of this analysand faced with the fact that the woman in question trusts the analyst, and the analysand probably has the lifestyle (and now this is my fantasy) of a Pharaoh? Impotence with the woman who has recommended the analyst to him? So, to the extent that the analyst is potent in the analysis, this risk of negative therapeutic reaction can lead to a problem of twinning in the transference. That is to say, what may appear as a blessing coming from the analyst is a curse, and what could be a curse is a blessing for the patient. If the analyst does not give up — and the analyst appears to have sufficient vitality to put up with the innumerable curses of a Pharaoh — the problem remains.

AUDIENCE: This material seems to contain three dreams by the patient: the dream of the insect trapped against the window pane; the dream of the swimming pools; and the dream of the arrest. I'd like to ask whether it might not be better for the analyst, as he performs his task of interpretation, to focus on the more visual elements of the patient, given that they trigger his dream.

AUDIENCE: The crucial point in clarifying the session seems to be the question of the patient's desire to stop time. I wonder whether this patient has an idea of time. Perhaps there is something prior to his ability and desire to control and stop time, something connected to inexistence, to the poor functioning of an α function relative to the perception of time. It seems to me that, technically speaking, from the point of view of interpreting the session, this might be a change of vertex.

DR FERRO: Thank you for your comments. Now, I would like to think about this more globally. I think there is an artistic capacity in the analyst, and that these intuitive images, that correspond to the α element, frequently form inside him. I must say that patients very often do this quite naturally. This morning,[1] I remembered a patient who, after an interpretation I had given her and which seemed to me adequate, was briefly silent, and then said: "Ah, today, at hospital I saw a child in A&E who had eaten some nails", expressing her reaction to what I had regarded as a good interpretation. Patients have this artistic ability to tell us how they experience our interpretations.

This process occurs on both sides, and it is not only the analyst who is capable of being creative and able to form images, α elements, from small projective identifications; patients do it all the time as well. The problem for the analyst is how to use the images, both those coming from the patient and his own, because decoding is not enough. If I had said to my patient that she had experienced what I said to her as stinging and scathing, she might have said that on television she had seen an elephant running into a crowd. If I had insisted and said, "You perceive what I told you as an act of violence etc.", she would simply not have come to the next session, perhaps with the excuse: "I've got earache". And if I had still kept on — "The things I have told you have made your ears sore" — then she wouldn't have come back for a week.

1 See Clinical Seminar II.

The question is, then, what type of transformation should we carry out in our way of relating to the patient? I agree that the central problem is one of communication, but it is also a question of how to communicate our images to the patient, in their words; what type of story to use to dissolve the images so that the patients can assimilate them as growth factors, and not as persecution factors.

In *Learning from Experience*,[2] Bion says that an excessively complex thought, which exceeds the containing powers of the apparatus for thinking thoughts, is evacuated as if it were an $\alpha$ element. So it is important that the analyst's interpretations do not go beyond the patient's ability to take them on board.

I agree with the point about the Pharaoh of Egypt, and this was the fantasy I had too, when I said that there was something mythical about the situation. I was thinking of the seven years of famine and the seven years of plenty. This also coincides with what has been said about not knowing time. I remembered that when the Pharaoh died, everybody had to die and, when the Pharaoh was buried, the people had to be buried with him. The narcissistic aspect of this patient is, I think, central because he experiences his own death as a cosmic catastrophe. In some respects, this is what happens to all of us, but only to a certain extent. I agree with the Pharaoh element and I would suggest that the first move should be to open the doors and to accept this terrible catastrophic anguish about death.

In this vein, in reply to the question about the patient's notion of time, I would say that we do not know what time means for the patient, but equally we do not know what death means for him. Undoubtedly it is not the biological aspect of death, but something that has to do with a nameless catastrophe. Thus our way of talking to him of the anguish of time etc. is a way of beginning to narrate something about an unknown thing that terrifies him. It is a way of being able to put a name to a primitive anguish, which we cannot see from this patient's perspective; that is to say, a nameless terror.

I agree with the idea of the three dreams. When the patient provides visual images, he is giving us something rich in $\alpha$ elements. It is as if the patient were the director and we were the

2 Bion, W. R. 1962. *Learning from Experience*. London: Heinemann.

editor of the film. Or perhaps our role is to touch up the editing on a film that has already been completed.

The work is more difficult when the patient does not give us any α elements but makes projective identifications, which we used to call evacuative or violent, but which are evacuative or violent viewed against our capacity to transform them into images. Transference dreams can help us in this respect. With particularly severe patients, I have often found myself engulfed and full of anguish without being able to organize this terrible anguish during the session. Then I would dream during the night, and through this dream I would be able to reorganize what had entered the session as violent projective identification. In this sense, the night-time dreams of the analyst have an important reparative function for the analyst's mind.

# Clinical Seminar I

ANALYST IN SUPERVISION: The patient was first referred to me by a day hospital, in March 1989, at the age of three and a half. He had been attending the day hospital for three months, where he had been diagnosed as autistic. He has been coming for seven years.

When they first approached me, the parents said that he was a strange, quiet child, who did not communicate or reply when spoken to, and who did not recognize his own name or look at people. At times, he gave the impression of not being able to hear and said only a few words, such as "Dad", "Mum", "Grandpa" and "water". He did not form complete sentences, produced no spontaneous language but would repeat TV advertising jingles, such as those for Banco Itaù, Casas Bahia, Liquidacao Mappin and Globo Rural. He never used the word "I".

He seemed to live in a world of his own. He would sit for hours in front of the television or watch objects that moved, such as record players. Other times, he was extremely agitated and incapable of paying attention to anything. He would walk this way and that and make strange movements with his hands and arms. At times, he would cry, groan and give the impression of being desperate. On these occasions, both his parents would be desperate as well, not knowing what to do. He was afraid of birthday parties, he didn't understand what a present was, and if he was given a parcel he would never open it. He ate little, would only accept food that was doughy or liquid, never ate spontaneously and often vomited.

We started with four sessions a week. For the first two months there was absolutely no communication with me. He was not interested in toys and he would wander around the room, making strange movements with his hands and arms. Sometimes, he would stare at his hands for a long period, and at other times he would look distressed, sweat a lot, breathe heavily and walk around the room in a mood that swung from quiet to agitated. Occasionally, he would walk up to the wash-hand basin and start turning the tap on and off. He never replied to any of my questions and showed no sign of listening to what I was saying. As he walked around he would talk to himself, saying words such as Banco Itaù, Benespa, Liquidacao Mappin and Casas Bahia etc.

I observed him. I pointed out to him how strange the therapeutic situation was, since he did not know me, or whether he could trust me. I pointed out that he was turning the tap on and off, that the water was coming out and disappearing, and that I came out and disappeared as well. He showed no sign of having heard me. Sometimes, I stood next to him and imitated his gestures, and said to him: "What do you think R. can hear? What is R. trying to tell me?". But it was as if he hadn't heard me.

After two months, I realized that R. was beginning to watch me surreptitiously out of the corner of his eye, and occasionally he would venture a glance at the toys in the box, albeit very furtively. After several sessions, he came up to me, took me by the hand, led me to the box and pointed at a little horse. I picked up the horse. He took it out of my hand and started to wander around the room holding it in his hand. At the end of the session, when I told him it was time to leave, he kept hold of the toy and showed no sign of wanting to let it go. I said that perhaps he needed it as a reminder of me and that he could take it with him and bring it back the next day. I was surprised when he came back the next day with the horse, because until then I didn't know whether or not he could hear what I was saying.

At the end of May, the father asked to see me because he was having difficulty keeping up with the payments for the therapy. He said he had hoped his medical insurance would cover part of the cost, but as this wasn't the case he wanted to have an appointment with me. R. was present during the conversation.

The following day I found R. barefoot in the waiting room and he followed me into the room barefoot, holding his shoes in his hands. As he came through the door, he said. "Watch out, danger!".

I was very surprised. He started to wander around, very agitated, sweating profusely and making strange movements and groaning. After a quarter of an hour in this agitated state, his groans came to resemble someone humming a song, and I recognized a Christmas carol, which I then began to sing:

> I left my shoe at the garden window,
> Father Christmas left me my Christmas present.
> How does Father Christmas manage not to forget anyone?
> Rich or poor, the old man always comes.

When I started to sing, he looked at me in surprise. It was the first time he had looked at me. He stopped walking around the room, came up to me, and looked me in the eyes. When I stopped singing, he asked me to sing again, saying "I left ..." (the first words of the carol). So I sang it again, over and over, because he asked me to several times. I tried to talk to him, but he insisted I sing again. After repeating it many times, I said: "R. is telling me that he heard and understood perfectly the conversation between Luzia and Dad". I went on, saying that he was very worried and anxious because our work was in danger, that's why he had come in barefoot, because he wanted to leave the shoes at the garden window. I also said that he wanted to know if Luzia was a Father Christmas who wouldn't forget R., and if she would continue to look after him, whether he was rich or poor.

I don't know if you can image how I felt: I was surprised, I had goose pimples, and although I hadn't the slightest idea how he was feeling, it was still a very exciting moment. Then R. took me by the hand, led me to the waiting room and pushed me towards his father. I told R. that he was very anxious, that he wanted the situation with his father to be resolved at once. I also said that I had arranged an appointment for the weekend and that I expected him to come the following day as usual.

The father watched us with an astonished look on his face, without understanding anything.

For me, this first communication by R. was surprising, unexpected and moving. I was pleased, and thought that the first step had been made. Up to then we had had fifty sessions. I thought that from now on the prognosis for R. was good. When I started to treat him, I didn't know whether the work would be possible, which is why we decided on a temporary contract. I agreed with the father that we would work for three months and then discuss how to go on. From that moment onwards, R. began to communicate with me through songs. We spent the next two months singing. R. began to sing with me, at first only one or two words, then each time a bit more. He didn't let me speak very much; he asked me to sing all the time, and I sang so much I got a sore throat. But when he spoke I paid careful attention. Then he started to use the words of the songs to speak, and he would repeat my words.

Every day when he arrived I followed a never-changing ritual to make things easier. I would say: "Hello R., how are you?". After a while he would come up to me and say: "Hello R., how are you?". Or, at the moment of leaving, I would say to him: "See you tomorrow". And he would say the same thing: "See you tomorrow".

His language was developing rapidly and in a surprising way. His parents felt happy and confident about the future. They reported to me that R. had not only started to talk but now would come up to them and ask them to do things. We were all so enthusiastic that we upped the number of sessions to five a week. Later, R. came up with a new song ("Sereno"):

Dew, I fall, I fall
Dew, let fall
The dawn dew
has not let my love sleep.

For the first time with this song, R. started to play a game with me. He would sit on my lap, ask me to sing the song and then he would slip off my lap, fall to the floor and burst into tears; a flood of tears.

The game was repeated numerous times and I told him that he was telling me a sad story, about a child falling and hurting himself and that he needed help so as not to carry on falling and hurting himself.

In the game I changed the words of the song:

Dew, I fall, I fall
Dew, do not let me fall

The dawn dew
does not let my R. fall.

R. laughed for the first time and seemed to like this game a lot, so we went on playing it until the end of the year.

On his return from the holidays the game of singing and falling from my lap was expanded to include a second part in which he strangled me. I spoke to him about the anger he felt when we separated and I "dropped" him. (The strangulation gesture was frightening: he would put his hands round my throat and put all his strength into it. The effort would screw up his face, but he never hurt me.)

R. developed a very strong bond with me and suffered greatly during holidays and at weekends. He started calling me "Banco Itaù", and for a long time I couldn't understand why.

One day I arrived at my studio and found R. desperate and in tears; he was calling for his father, who wasn't there. In the midst of all this convulsive crying, he asked me: "do you do vaccines?".

He said he wanted to tell me about having had a vaccine; that he had been very frightened; that he had needed me and I wasn't there. Gradually, he calmed down, went out of the room and picked up a magazine and showed me an ad for Banco Itaù. The slogan was "Banco Itaù, the electronic bank: the bank that is there for you when you need it". He pointed at the ad, and then asked: "Does the Banco Itaù bite?".

Then I said to him that he felt that I bit, that I was bad when I wasn't there when he needed me. I said he needed a psychologist who was a Banco Itaù.

From then on, R. would come in and tell me about the state of the Stock Exchange, which astonished me. For a few days I decided to note down the figures he gave. Later, I checked them and discovered that they were right. This was the period when Governor Collor was in power and everything was in great turmoil. R. had already repeated various things he had heard on television during the election campaign, and the people who appeared every day on TV seemed to keep him calm. He particularly liked Afif Domingos, who had a campaign ditty about hope. When the election and the political advertising came to an end, he was desperate; he kept on asking where the people had gone.

When Collor took power, he tightened the money supply and nobody knew whether to go to work or not. Everything was in chaos. R. suffered a lot; he had the fantasy I might disappear, like the candidates on TV.

Later, R. began to repeat a telephone number and to knock on my door. It took me some time to work out where the number came from: it was the number of the CVV (the Samaritans), which people phoned when they were desperate and contemplating suicide. Little by little I understood that he wanted me to say that he could come in when he knocked on the door, and that I wouldn't abandon him in moments of despair.

It was during this period (about a year and a half after the beginning of the therapy) that his parents told me that they were thinking of having another child. R. was their only child and they were afraid they might have another autistic child, but now they were more certain that they did want another child.

R. began to come out with fantasies about this possible brother or sister. He talked about thieves, policemen, murderers; he talked about removing the calendar from his parents' room; and also about falling and hurting himself. I spoke to him about his desire to know what happened in the parents' bedroom; how babies were born; his fear of losing his place because of the brother-thief; and his anger at the possible brother or sister he didn't want, or who he wanted to kill.

R.'s aunt, his mother's sister, was pregnant at the time and he spoke a lot about surrogate mothers. At the time there was a TV soap opera with this title, and he thought that this child would be his brother or sister. But then, in the sixth month of pregnancy, his aunt lost her baby. This was followed by a paranoid period that went on for about four or five months.

One time, R. came into the room, took the toy cart and buried it in a little garden that is part of my room. After burying it, he heard the siren from a police car that was, in fact, passing by at that moment, and started to shout for help, saying that the police were looking for him. A few moments later, he came closer to me, hid behind me and asked me to protect him from the police. At other times, he ran away from me saying that I was going to report him to the police. He remained in this state of confusion for several months.

It was a difficult period: there were times when he didn't want to come in; other times when he didn't want to go out. And he would often ask me, where is Luzia? Because I wasn't Luzia; I was a witch dressed up as Luzia, and I had locked Luzia up somewhere.

He got over this episode and some months later his mother became pregnant. Then R. went back to being very anxious and told me that his parents were mad. At that point he was speaking relatively well.

I said that, in his opinion, his parents were mad to have another child because he thought he would become so furious and jealous as to want to kill them. I said that in my view, however, the parents were not mad and trusted in his ability to control himself, and that I trusted him too. He calmed down and we spent months working on his confusion between thought and action. He felt more relieved, and prepared himself to welcome the arrival of his sister more calmly (by now they knew that it was going to be a baby girl).

The baby sister was born, and during the whole of 1993, we worked on the theme of jealousy: the fear that B. would steal his place; the fear that I would treat B. and not him; fantasies that other people might want to hurt B. One day he told me: "In the lift somebody wanted to harm my sister and I defended her". He repeated this very often.

Sometimes, when the mother brought R. to the session, she also brought B., but he wouldn't let me come close to her, on the pretext that I might hurt her. We worked a lot on projections and on how he was confused by not knowing who felt what.

After two years, R. started to be more stable in his behaviour; he no longer experienced intense states of disorganization, or cold sweats, fear or stomach ache. He no longer experienced states of great confusion. He is now ten years old and is in the third year of a normal school. He has no difficulty in keeping up with the class. In the middle of last year he managed to start doing joined-up writing, whereas previously he had written letters separately, and thought he was incapable of joining up letters. He takes part in group activities, excursions outside school, has a good vocabulary and gets on very well with adults, who always appreciate him. But he doesn't get on with children, especially with boys. The boys make fun of him, swear and provoke him, and up to a year ago, R. put up with this without reacting. Some months ago he started to react, but always under great suffering. He experiences any argument as extremely dangerous. Despite all his progress, R. is a child who is strange and different. His language is unimaginative and moralistic; he comes across as a priest giving a sermon. He repeats the same thing many times.

For some time now, I have felt that the work is proceeding very slowly: he gets stuck for months, then he picks up a little, moves on, but then gets stuck again. I feel that R. is avoiding any real in-depth exploration and is asking me to stay on the surface. I chose to talk about this case because, for some time now, I feel somewhat lost. After evolving so well, things have now come to a halt. I don't know whether this is because he has reached his limit, or because he is going through the latency period, or because I am the one who has got lost.

For a few months he has been playing hangman. He protests against his friends who swear and provoke him. He says that swearing is very nasty, it shows a lack of good manners, that God doesn't like it, and that the boys do it because they are envious of him because he is good, intelligent and well-behaved. R. never replies to questions and is highly evasive all the time. I imagine that this is one of the difficulties he has in getting on with other children. Now I shall describe a session.

*R. arrives with his nose bleeding and his t-shirt covered in blood. He shows me his bloody clothes and says he's going to the bathroom to wash them. He comes back five minutes later, holding a piece of toilet paper under his nose, which is still dripping blood.*

ANALYST: What have you done to your nose?
PATIENT: Nothing. I'm very happy!
ANALYST: What do you mean? I don't understand.
PATIENT: Do you know I have had a nice day?

*I feel lost. R. is reticent and appears to want to change the subject.*

ANALYST: Why don't you want to talk about what has happened to your nose?
PATIENT: It's nothing. This happens all the time. The doctor told me that this always happens when people run around a lot, when they jump and are happy. Don't be sad. Everything is okay.

*(I think that, at that time, when he lived in a state of anxiety, other people would often say this to him. So when he was upset he said to himself: "Don't be sad. Everything is okay.")*

PATIENT: Did you know that my mother has dyed her hair blonde?

*I am puzzled because I saw his mother briefly when she brought him to the session, and her hair was its normal brown colour. I realize that R. didn't know I had seen his mother briefly. Then I try to say:*

ANALYST: Perhaps you are trying to tell me that something has changed in your mother's head.

*He doesn't let me finish and says:*

PATIENT: No, that's not it. You don't understand. I'm telling you that she has dyed her hair blonde.
ANALYST: Luzia used to be blonde ... *(I am trying ...)*
PATIENT: You don't understand me. Why don't you understand me? Shall we go and play hangman?

*He goes up to the board and gets things ready. He has great difficulty preparing the game, but he indicates the number of letters. The word was "tortoise" and I guessed it.*

PATIENT: How did you guess that? Now it's your turn.

*I suggest the word "hiding place" (I thought to myself that I might be a tortoise, because the tortoise has a shell to hide behind. So I put "hiding place".)*

*He starts getting the letters wrong, and as he gets closer to being hanged, he gets anxious and starts to sweat and his voice sounds like he is about to cry. He speaks in a disjointed way.*

PATIENT: Oof, I don't like losing. Why are you doing this? It's very difficult ... I don't want to be hanged! I'll tell you everything about my mother! There's the letter "T" ... no, there isn't ... You can't hang me, I know it's not there ... There's the letter "T" ... no ... You mustn't hang me! ... I can't think ... It's very difficult, I don't want to be hanged!

*I realize that he can't think straight, so I say:*

ANALYST: You are as anguished as if it were a real gallows and not a game. I think you feel that I am proposing very dangerous things and words that might hurt you.

*(Writing the word, I realize that "tortoise" might refer to moving slowly and that that hadn't occurred to me. Perhaps using the word "hiding place" meant not respecting his request to go slowly.)*

PATIENT: Why don't you understand anything?

ANALYST: I'm trying, but I can see that I'm not having much success. Apparently, you think I am doing it deliberately, that I'm just being nasty, that I no longer want to be at your side.

*After this intervention, R. calms down and manages to guess the word "hiding place" before being hanged. Then he chooses the word "feeling", which I guess.*

PATIENT: How did you manage to get that? You know everything, don't you, Luzia?

ANALYST: Apparently, there's something very important that I don't know at the moment: how to help you.

*R. raises his arms, twists them and starts to shout for help, saying that he is trapped, that he can't get out, and he asks me to help him.*

*I start to speak, but he insists, and shouts in great anguish. So I go up to him and (literally) unravel his arms. Then he seems satisfied.*

ANALYST: You're telling me that you're imprisoned and coiled up, that you need my help to be freed. How can I help you?

*R. repeats this game another two times and it is important to him that I go up to him and literally unravel him. Then he goes to the board and plays a new round of hangman with the word "anger". When I work out the word, I say:*

ANALYST: I think you're giving me a clue to help you: has it got something to do with anger?

*Then he writes the word "dive" and says that he wants to give me a clue. There's a remedy for the pain. At this point I look at the clock and say that the hour is up, and he leaves.*

AUDIENCE: What does the boy look like?

ANALYST IN SUPERVISION: He is a very good-looking boy. He is big for his age, has an absent-minded air and is constantly touching some part of his body; for example, his navel. There is always some part of his body that is uncovered. But he is a very attractive boy.

AUDIENCE: Strange?

ANALYST IN SUPERVISION: There's something different about him that people notice. It's nothing really strange but he's visibly different.

DR FERRO: I'm thinking that I would like to say "tortoise" too, to make you go more slowly, because the material is very rich, very dense, very lively. I would like to listen a little, to know what the people in the audience are thinking, to have a bit more time to understand the material. Not just opinions, but also any fantasies and impressions any of you might have.

ANALYST IN SUPERVISION: What I have recounted is a summary of almost seven years. It's difficult to sum up seven years, and rereading what I have written I realize that I have left out some important things, but I couldn't write any more. I think it is important to say that there was a time when he used to write little notes: he used to say the letters (he was already able to spell at the age of four and a half), and I would write for him. They were notes riddled with holes, such as "R. was born at the São Paulo Maternity hospital in Rua Frei Caneca ...". The next note: "R.'s first address was at such and such a street". Then he left me a photo of when he was a babe in arms, and he asked me to keep the photo together with the pierced notes. Later, he wrote the name of his first school and the second house where he lived. I thought that he was compiling a kind of childhood diary with me. I have kept these pages, and every now and then he asks me where they are and wants to see them.

When I started preparing my account of this case, I had to think of myself and I realized that I had certain desires towards my patient. I find him brilliant and I have never resigned myself to this slow rate of progress. As I was writing I realized that perhaps I should have slowed down and not proceeded according to my desires. Needless to say, I was disappointed when he said that I didn't understand anything.

AUDIENCE: I really like the way you worked with him and the way you presented the case. The story of the diary gives me the impression that he had a psychological birth seven years ago, and that he is entering a period of latency and his pace is that of a tortoise. He is behind time and he says it to make you understand the difficulty he has with games which are typical of seven- or eight-year-old children. My seven- or eight-year-old patients play hangman. The tortoise then represents his rhythm; he is ten years old but emotionally seven. It is very difficult working in this period because of all the difficulties of latency. What's more, there is the desire to be a ten-year-old child, but I think that you worked very well with him, you presented the case well. It was very touching.

AUDIENCE: How does he react to holidays and interruptions?

ANALYST IN SUPERVISION: The last two years, he has been reasonably calm. Before that, when he came back, he would be absolutely out of his mind. During our first two years of work, I would only go on trips to nearby places, and even during my holidays I would come back to have at least one session a week with him. After two years, I decided that this was no longer necessary. I started going on longer holidays and he would come back to me in a poor state: the mother told me that he was ill, that he had a temperature, bronchitis. Lately, however, he has started to react well.

AUDIENCE: When did you start noticing that he would say things like "You don't understand me?". Does it coincide with the time when you had the impression of "arrest?".

ANALYST IN SUPERVISION: Yes, it does. I thought of lots of things when I was writing up the sessions to present here. I thought he had stabilized, and that for him things were fine; in short, that he had got over the state of atrocious distress he used to have. But he had stabilized on a low level, in a less intelligent, less brilliant way, and showing fairly split-off behaviour: "I am good, I am good-looking, I am intelligent, the hurt is all over there". He rejected all the interpretations I made that were designed to reintegrate him, and which were part of this phase: "You don't understand me, I don't want to talk about that". At the moment, he is much better than before but he is not trying to make progress; at least, for the moment.

AUDIENCE: Do you think it is a reaction to this attempt at reintegration?

ANALYST IN SUPERVISION: I don't even know whether it is reintegration, or whether he is now starting to integrate. Working with autistic children creates a lot of anxiety, because they get better but sometimes the improvements resemble getting worse. They may start to have hallucinations for no apparent reason, and although this is an improvement, all the parents see is their child having hallucinations and they get frightened. There are improvements that look suspicious and sometimes I ask even myself: "Is this an improvement or a deterioration?". It's a process where you constantly ask yourself questions.

AUDIENCE: I am thinking about your perception of an arrested process. The sister isn't autistic, is she?

ANALYST IN SUPERVISION: No.

AUDIENCE: In his own head, he must be well aware, through the parents, of the comparison between his sister's progress and his probable "arrest". My view is that up to now he has had no term of comparison in the family, and perhaps he would have wanted to discuss it with you.

ANALYST: I'll think about it.

AUDIENCE: I've had a subjective impression which has little justification, but is nonetheless very strong: the two songs drew my attention to it — "Sereno" and "Shoe at the garden window" — because of the refrain they both have. In this ten-year-old child I sense the aggressiveness, the lulling movement, which has remained throughout your relationship. I can't really explain what I mean. I'm talking about a very subjective impression.

AUDIENCE: I would like to compliment you on your rapidity, which is at the opposite extreme to the patient's rate of progress. How can someone so fast accompany a tortoise? But what took my attention is that even from the first information you gave us there were clear-cut characteristics of obsessive-compulsive disorder (turning taps on and off, and other repeated actions), which are psychic representations without emotional content. Congratulations on the evolution of the patient, on your work, because he has progressively abandoned this obsessive-compulsive profile and moved on to have psychic representations with an affective content, to the point of using the word "feeling".

ANALYST IN SUPERVISION: I would like to say something as well, as it seems that everybody has the impression I have been too fast. There are moments when I stop to write some notes about R. and I reflect on them and think: he has taken three months to come out of this phase of primary autism and start a communication; he has spent something like a year and a half in a symbiotic phase with me. The following phase would be schizoid-paranoid, and we have been in the schizoid-paranoid phase for four years. Of these four years, two have been productive, and it seems to me that we have been bogged down during the other two. So I think if he has come this far, why can't he get out of it? Because there are no signs of the characteristics of the depressive phase.

DR FERRO: I'll start with some impressions, but I think that half an hour is not enough for such rich material; we would need to talk about it all day long. I would distinguish between various phases. The first is the phase of resuming contact with the child. I recall an adult patient of mine who had a degree. After two or three years of analysis, she said to me: "When my boyfriend talks to me about something, I don't pay the slightest attention to the words he uses. I try to understand from the tone of voice if he loves me that day or not".

I think that in the first phase there is a massive evacuation of β elements, through the stereotypes, the movements, the crying fits, which represent a mechanism of absolute evacuation. It is as if the other person were perceived as someone incapable of receiving and digesting — like the television; something not receptive, without an internal space. It is clear that from the beginning he prefers food that is either in liquid or blended form, he vomits readily, almost as if he were unable to absorb and digest, but could only be fed with minimal things.

I think that, in the first phase of therapy, the child has no understanding of content. In the beginning, it is more or less as if we were talking about logarithms to a primary school child, which does not mean that the analyst should not refer to content, but in this phase, the child cannot have access to this content. He is perfectly able to register the rhythm, the music, the affective quality and the availability of the analyst, to let his anxieties and β elements pass through him.

We can understand how the transformation of β elements on the part of the analyst occurs when she begins to activate a process of symbolization: in this joint-stock company the patient's capital is very small, 20–30 per cent, whereas the analyst puts in 70–80 per cent, transforming what comes from the patient in an imprecise and open manner into images and fantasies. When, for example, there was a threat of suspending the therapy, I don't think that he understood exactly what it meant, but he must have been seized by great anxiety. This is what he experienced at that moment, and that's what we have to work with.

There is a big difference between working on and working with the process of symbolization. Symbolization presupposes that what the patient brings along already has a meaning — and that it is up to the analyst to decode this meaning. In the process of symbolization, on the other hand, there is no pre-existing meaning: there is a new two-person construction in the session.

I really like the communication that is established through music: it begins with a moan then modulates into a melody, and then words are added. The meanings begin to appear with "serene", when he senses that his anxieties are accepted and can be cleared up by another person.

Another important passage is when the first structured game begins: when he asks the analyst to take him on her lap, the two start singing, he slips, falls and cries. This is, in effect, the beginning of their relationship as a couple. It is the starting point for the analyst's dream, when he says: "A sad story of a child who falls and hurts himself and needs help, so that he can avoid falling in future". At this moment, an emotional grammar between the two is created.

It is an important point of departure because, from this moment on, the problems arise: the possibility of an emotional fabric forming between the two of them allows very violent proto-emotions to come to the fore. This reminds me of Bion when he talks about the development of content and the development of the container. It is as if we had, from this moment on, a proliferation of proto-emotions, which no longer have sufficient opportunity to be transformed and thought. It is as if, from this moment on, the child made more reference to the need for a claustrum; as if these proto-emotions were so intense, so galloping, so violent that, if it was not possible to transform them within the work of the couple, they might at least be contained within the shell of the tortoise.

What I find remarkable, throughout the first part of the therapy, is this capacity to enter into contact with the child, and to give him back access to words and emotions.

It seems to me that at some point there is a break, in the sense that there is a lot of focus on the external story. Perhaps it would be more fruitful to address the internal story of the sessions, and all the violent emotions that have been activated inside the session by facts that have to do with the relationship. Also, the information about President Collor, who had taken power and frozen all bank accounts, leaving all therapies in mid-air, hanging on a thread, seems to be a communication of something which happens inside the session: as if the child thought that up to a certain point there was someone capable of looking after his emotions and needs, but now he wondered whether there was anybody capable of dealing with his more violent and uncontrollable side.

As to the parents' question — whether it was crazy for them to think of having another child — rather than looking at this from a real point of view (which, of course, exists), I think of the child's worries that a violent, uncontrolled part of him will enter the consulting room; a part that contains anger, violence and conflict with the analyst.

ANALYST IN SUPERVISION: He was the one who wrote the word "anger".

DR FERRO: He says that swearing is a sign of bad manners and that God doesn't like children who do that, as if there were an affectionate and loving part of this child which has been recognized, and has entered into contact with the analyst. It is only that — thanks to this capacity of the analyst to establish an emotional contact with the child — an emotional fabric has been woven, which has generated inside him a proliferation of proto-emotional aspects that, previously, had been absolutely unthinkable.

I think that at this point in the therapy the child is afraid that the analyst has changed and no longer has the same head: "My mother has changed the colour of her hair". It is as if he were afraid that his analyst — who is the person who has given him the word, who has given him the capacity to feel, the capacity to experience emotions — might consider it inappropriate to have proto-emotional stories, to talk of bloody stories. Like the blood which the child completely denies at the beginning of the session. He says: "Blood comes out when people are happy and jump around", as if he were afraid that the bloody stories could not be told and commented on with the analyst. When he says to the analyst: "You don't understand me, you never understand me", he can say it because up to that point the analyst had, in fact, understood him very well, but now he needs to make a decisive qualitative leap, towards more violent contents.

At any rate, I think that the tortoise refers in some way to the claustrum where these proto-emotions are to be found, before new songs can be discovered. There is an Italian singer, Ornella Vanoni, who for a long time sang songs about the "*mala*" (criminal underworld). We need to move on from songs about Father Christmas and serenity to songs of blood, but always at the pace of a tortoise. And now, using the same extraordinary capacity that the analyst had at the beginning, the analyst needs to hope that the meanings can be shared by the couple without saturating the violent aspects brought to the fore by interpretations of content, trusting that the inspiration for blood songs will come.

The violence is not only in the patient or in his emotions towards the analyst, but — as the analyst herself says at one point — also the analyst's words can be dangerous and cause suffering. So the most important point lies not in interpreting these aspects of violence but in transforming aspects of violence and blood into a song the couple can share, in the same way as they did with the songs about Father Christmas and serenity, where one composes the melody and the other writes the words. It is as if we had to pass from Christmas carols to heavy metal. That's when the question of anger appears.

AUDIENCE: I would appreciate it if you could go into the session in more depth.

DR FERRO: I have tried to sum up the content of the session. There almost seems to be a discrepancy between the first scene and the rest. It is as if we were watching a film or a play, and right at the beginning a character appears covered in blood. Immediately, we imagine this is going to be a violent film, set in the Bronx. But then immediately a Walt Disney type film starts, as if the blood story had started but had then been halted with a lie, putting it in Column Two in Bion's Grid.

The analyst is ready to investigate, but it is as if there is some kind of terror of these deeper and more violent aspects. There is the child's terror that the mother has changed and wants to gild everything, or wants to see everything gilded, and his terror that he cannot bring blood to this blonde-haired mother. There is a blonde, gilded story in which everything is fine; the nose bleeds when you are happy. And there is a *noir* story which lies underneath, and not only appears at the moment of blood but also in the story of the hangman, which can be seen not as a children's game but as this violent level coming to the fore. There seem to be two films: one by Walt Disney and the other starring Charles Bronson. We have only seen a couple of scenes of the Charles Bronson movie: the blood, the gallows, and perhaps some other moment that escapes me; perhaps, the hiding place, the request for help. The point is to allow this Charles Bronson to emerge, to strip off the Walt Disney veneer, which stops the other film from emerging.

AUDIENCE: It is the child himself who suggests that the blood appears at moments when people play, have fun, are happy, and this means that he understands that these two films are in communication with each other and that when he lives, when he plays, bleeding occurs.

DR FERRO: For the moment we don't know what the blood means that comes out of the Charles Bronson film; it could be connected to separations, to jealousy or to violence. Now we need to find a good director, like the excellent director we had at the beginning of the analysis. We need a Fritz Lang or a Sergio Leone to direct this second film that is waiting to be made.

AUDIENCE: The child makes a symbolic equation when he draws the gallows and when, some sessions earlier, he plays at strangling the analyst.

DR FERRO: I don't exactly remember what happened in the session, what happened in the story, but the hangman game allows a transitional space to form: "Let's see if you are afraid of this or if we can start to talk of violence and the gallows while playing". The child's great fear is that Charles Bronson might emerge from the game, escape from the film and really strangle the analyst. In this sense, there is a proliferation of content which must be imprisoned, because his fear is that it may not be contained within the film.

Do you remember the film with Woody Allen where the characters come out of the film and enter the auditorium? In Column Two of the Grid, where lies are to be found, it is like putting a glass pane in front of the film to make sure Charles Bronson doesn't escape. I don't see Charles Bronson as something bad, but as something that has to do with intense proto-emotions.

AUDIENCE: The analyst talks about suggesting this pane of glass to the patient when she said: "I am certain your parents are not mad, I am certain that you can understand all this". I would like to put the following question: would it be necessary through this understanding to make up for the moment when the analyst fails to address these 'Charles Bronson' contents, or is it possible to let the analysis proceed and accept them in a new way?

DR FERRO: I would always see this in terms of the analytic couple; it is not the analyst who inserts the first pane of glass, and then the patient who does the same. At some point there is the fear that it is necessary to insert the pane of glass to stop Charles Bronson getting out. Thank goodness defences have been invented; Column Two. We cannot always be in what Bion terms "a state of

O" with the patient. It is a defensive movement: "You manage to control yourself; your parents are not mad".

But this is where the question of madness comes up: "You have taught me to communicate, but together can we also see the madness of the emotions? Can we address this?".

I think that the analyst should turn up to the session with a punk haircut.

# Clinical Seminar II

Analyst in supervision: At the first interview João complained that nothing in his life was working; in particular, he mentioned his studies and his work. He was twenty-two years old and was in his first year of Mechanical Engineering. The strong impression I had of him from the first interview was that he was like a bush that had been torn from the ground, whose roots were showing and which was now in search of a new place to be planted. There were signs of violence and damage in him which were covered over by joviality, cheerfulness and a constant good mood. João agreed with everything, or almost everything: changes to our timetable, sessions being cancelled. He rarely disagreed with what I said. As time passed, I made new observations and gained further impressions: João had a tendency, which I called "compulsion to repair", or, in his own words, a "mania to repair everything". This applied especially to cars, which he adored, but also extended to any broken object around the house that belonged to his *family* in the broadest sense of the word, but also to his analyst.

Once, during the first month of analysis, on entering the room, João jumped on to the chair next to the desk to repair one of the blinds that was askew, and had been for months. It was an almost imperceptible defect; he fixed it quickly and was clearly very proud of his work. In addition to this reparative tendency, with its evident defensive colouring, he also prompted in me the impression of dismantlement or quartering, as if he were in pieces and trying to survive an explosion. Several times I thought of the figure of Frankenstein's monster, and the efforts he made to become human. I thought, too, of the vicissitudes and tragedies involved in this process, both his emotional and creative possibilities and his monstrosity.

At the beginning of each session, João often twists around on the couch. The movements he makes are quite distinctive and similar to stretching. He squeezes the cushion with great vigour, often leaving it so crumpled that the cover has to be changed. Sometimes he crosses his legs and almost touches the wall with the soles of his shoes. These observations suggest that something will soon erupt.

In general, even at the beginning of the session, when he is not saying anything, he lets out a rather low sound. This meowing-like noise is reminiscent of a cat asking to be stroked. As a rule, it is difficult to talk and to get the session started. His attachment to the concrete world of objects, cars and things is very strong. The rudimentary mechanical aspects of things force their way into what he is saying. For him things and objects are possible words. The psychical world — dreams, feelings, the possibility of getting excited — seem to be miles away.

For two years, João has been coming to sessions regularly, four times a week. He occasionally misses a session but, in general, he makes sure that he lets the analyst know in advance, saying things like "I would like to warn you that today I can't make it".

The emotional atmosphere of the analytic bond could be called *ambivalent*. Once he said: "It doesn't matter whether I come or not". On another occasion he said: "If my father stopped me from doing analysis, it would be annoying, but there's nothing I could do about it". Another day, however, he said: "I don't know why, but it does me good to make conversation with you".

His feeling of abandonment is transferred on to material, concrete complaints about things such as cars, meals, presents, bookshelves. João is the child of separated parents. He lived with his mother up to the age of seventeen, at which point, after a number of conflicts, he decided to leave and live with his father.

He complained about the cold and distant relationship he had with his parents; he was always in a state of waiting for some external movement of approach from them. His mother died some years ago, an event that did not change the atmosphere of distance and anaesthesia. João referred to her as possessive and rigid, someone who did not tolerate her child's development and independence. She also constantly left him with various nannies.

He sees the father as negligent, and does not forgive him for having handed him over to his mother after their separation. The parents lost another child a few months before he was born.

He experiences love and establishing a relationship as a danger to be avoided and to deny violently. This leads me to think he engages in a kind of anaesthesia to avoid suffering, mental pain. João has had a girlfriend for several years. The image suggested by his relationship with her is that of a buoy to which João clings desperately, holding on by his fingernails and teeth so as not to drown in a wild and dark sea. At times, he expresses his intention to live with his girlfriend one day, but he always sees this as an event belonging to a distant and unreachable future, and this is a source of continual conflict between them. There is a dimension in his life of eternal waiting, which comes out in the existential paralysis about which João complains. He seems to deny the temporal dimension with great violence. This waiting suggests that he is waiting, simultaneously, for a tragedy or a miracle. It is as if João thinks there is something wrong with him, something broken that cannot be fixed. So the solution is to wait for death so as to be born again.

When I suggested to him the model of the ugly duckling which waited for nature to transform it into a beautiful adult swan, he replied: "I don't know, but I think I'll stay as the ugly duckling for ever".

On another occasion, I mentioned the model of the prince that knows that one day he will be crowned, and is waiting for his father to die so that he can become king. In the meantime, his life is transformed into a period of waiting to ascend the throne; in some ways, waiting for death. João listens carefully to what I say and then says: "You know, I've never thought about it. It may take a long time for the king to die. I do not know why I can't do anything. I'm waiting for the others to decide and I do nothing. It's been a year since I left university and I haven't done anything. A.B. *(his girlfriend)* gets on at me and says that if I go on like this we'll never get married".

I shall describe two sessions. The first took place in October 1995, after more or less one year of analysis.

*The secretary tells me that the patient has arrived and I go to get him.*

PATIENT: I've got to make a phone call. I'll be up in a moment.

*I say that he can come up when he's done, I'll be waiting for him. I waited about fifteen minutes, during which time I found myself faced with an empty couch and asked myself: "Why does João leave his place empty? What stops him from occupying his place in life?"*

*At the end of this period of waiting, the patient arrived, threw himself on the couch and said:*

PATIENT: Sorry, I'm very late, but I had to phone somebody from the insurance company. My policy expires tomorrow and I can't drive with an expired policy.

ANALYST: I just wanted to confirm that, as I said some weeks ago, next week I'll be away on business.

*The patient quickly makes himself comfortable on the couch and says:*

PATIENT: So tell me how much I owe you, I want to pay you.

ANALYST: You can pay me when I come back, on the 1st of November.

PATIENT: No. I'd prefer to pay before, otherwise I'll forget and we'll have the same mess as last week.

*(As far as I was concerned, there had been no mess; he had paid a little late, but it was nothing significant.)*

PATIENT: I don't want to leave things in mid-air.

*The expression "in mid-air" took my attention. It suggested to me an umbilical cord, something cut, an emblem of separation. And I say:*

ANALYST: You say that when I am away your analysis will remain in mid-air. There will be a cut between us.

PATIENT: No, not a cut, that's too strong an expression. It's only an interruption.

ANALYST: What kind of scales transform heavy into light? Perhaps for you my absence is not so light.

*The analyst is about to continue when he is interrupted.*

PATIENT: Ah! What do want me to do? Do you want me chain you up with a ball and chain like a prisoner?

ANALYST: If you tied me up, I couldn't go away, there would be no cut or interruption, would there?

*Five minutes of silence. The patient interrupts the silence and talks about his phone call.*

PATIENT: I was on the phone to sort out my insurance because it was about to expire, and my father only pays the insurance on the car, not on the accessories. In other words, I have to pay for the radio and the cassette recorder. My medical test is no longer valid. I wanted to sort everything out. My friend knows someone who does a medical test by appointment, and I wanted to see about it immediately.

ANALYST: Paying me in advance, as you say you want to do, serves as a kind of insurance policy; it guarantees my return. So what is heavy seems lighter.

*João laughs and says:*

PATIENT: That's an interesting idea. *(He doesn't go on.)*

*Another five minutes of silence, more or less.*

PATIENT: Yesterday afternoon, when my father arrived, I was in the garage talking to the driver. Do you know what happened? My father said "hello" from a distance and stayed to talk to the driver. I was furious. At lunchtime a conversation started about the insurance and I told him how things stood. I said: "Nobody pays my insurance. I do it". Later, my father knew I was angry. He came to me and, in order to please me, invited me to go to the motor show. That's the way I am. All I think about is cars and anybody can win me round that way.

ANALYST: I understand that you are anxious to be pleasant, likeable and joking with me, but perhaps in that way, in fact, you can't understand what you feel … or you put on the scales what is heavy and distinguish it from what is light.

*There is a silence and I say:*

ANALYST: So you cannot occupy your space.

PATIENT: Maybe, but what can I do to occupy the rest of the empty place?

ANALYST: I think that you understand that heavy feelings do not disappear with a magic wand. Perhaps you would like to talk about them here, to get angry, to become sad, to make demands, to complain, to argue, to get excited.

PATIENT: Yes, but you know that I can't do this anywhere. Sometimes, but only with my girlfriend. The other day was X's birthday *(his father's wife)* and I wanted A.B. to phone X. She didn't want to because she thinks they don't like her, but I told her to phone X. She didn't phone, but I told her what I wanted. I don't know why, but I never speak.

ANALYST: When one realizes what one feels and thinks, and doesn't disregard what is disturbing, the pain is greater. You are very afraid of feeling pain.

PATIENT: Ah yes, I really am! I want to be happy, look at things positively.

ANALYST: But there are things in life that are not positive.

PATIENT: Do you know what? I'm going to visit my mother; she's in hospital. I haven't spoken to her for a long time. I've hardly ever spoken to her since I left her house and went to live with my father. Even when we speak — for example, when it's her birthday — she seems like a different person. She doesn't seem to be my mother. The girl who was my nanny phoned me to tell me she was ill in hospital. She phoned so that I would go and see her.

ANALYST: This subject — oppressive feelings, things that are not positive — immediately reminded you of your mother, your relationship with her, her illness.

*Several minutes' silence.*

PATIENT: Yes, I always think it is better not to think about it.

*Further silence.*

ANALYST: Let's stop there for today.

The second session is from September 1996, after about two years of analysis.

*João arrives late, explaining that there had been problems with the traffic in the car park next to his new house.*

PATIENT: There were several cars parked behind mine and there was no space to get out. I had to do a thousand manoeuvres. *(He lies on the couch and continues talking about the new house.)* We still have no gas; we're still in the middle of moving, you have to adapt. We can't even eat. Yesterday, when I understood that there was nothing for lunch, I tried to get hold of my father so that we could have lunch together. I don't like being alone. *(He is silent and then goes on to talk about his father.)* I'm starting to realize that my father is worried about money. The people who bought his factory are not paying on time. I'm worried about my uncle. He is already old, and now that he has a problem with his prostate, he is urinating blood. I don't know when he's going to get out of hospital.

*What comes to mind is the sad image of a forest where pine trees are being re-planted. It reminds me of the silence of the forest and the absence of birds, which have to migrate to get food. The question of life and death enters the atmosphere of the session. I say:*

ANALYST: I think you are very afraid of dying of hunger when you are alone. Perhaps you think that food is always outside you.

*João understands my observation on the concrete level, and says:*

PATIENT: No, that's not it. I really don't like being alone.

ANALYST: You have the idea that life is movement and that movement is always in others, somewhere outside you. Perhaps you imagine that inside you there is no movement, there is congestion; like the congestion you found this morning in the car park.

*A silence of some minutes, then he resumes:*

PATIENT: Do you know I've got to adjust the main door to get my car in? I'll find a solution. I think that I'll use the same system as the door which opens from the inside.

*And he explains in great detail the machine he plans to install.*

ANALYST: If it's for opening the front door outwards, it seems that inside there is movement. There is congestion, but there are also openings.

PATIENT *(after a silence)*: The good thing about moving house is that the staff have started to appreciate me. I did everything: all the wiring, the lighting, the central heating, various other things. *(He makes a few comments about his important contribution to the move.)*

ANALYST: You are relieved to understand that there is heat, light, life in you, and that the others can see it as well.

PATIENT: Maybe. I don't know.

ANALYST: The closed door makes it impossible to enter into some unknown spaces. *(Then a memory of my own occurs to me: the cold room in our house that was closed all year round and was opened only to celebrate Easter.)* If the door remains barred, you are imprisoned in one space and unable to venture into others.

PATIENT: You know, I've always been like this. Ever since I was a child, I never liked being alone. I always went to sleep in my grandmother's bed. Also shortly before moving to my father's house, I went to sleep in my grandmother's bed. Right up to the time I moved to my father's house, I went to sleep in my grandmother's bed.

*At this moment I understand that some great sadness has formed.*

ANALYST: You are feeling sad at the moment.
PATIENT *(after a silence)*: I am thinking that the move is almost over and I'll have nothing to do.

*I sense in João an enormous fear of his inner emptiness and I find myself thinking of possible jobs for him. We are silent for some minutes. I say:*

ANALYST: I am thinking of an electronic plant with all the wires cut to avoid a short circuit. This image may help you to think that what you imagine is happening. If the wires are cut, there is no light or heat, not even a short circuit, no pain or suffering.

*João remains in silence. I continue:*

ANALYST: This image of the cut wires may give an impression of emptiness, of nothingness. But the cut wires are what actually exist.

*Again silence. I ask:*

ANALYST: What does this suggest to you?
PATIENT: That I should try to connect the wires, but it would be a lot of hard work.
ANALYST: Your repairing mania has something to do with this …
PATIENT: I thought of my uncle's boiler. When the problem came up, I thought I wouldn't be able to repair it. It was super-complicated; it was an old house, with old conductors, old bathroom fittings, a small trapdoor. In the end, I managed to get it done. It wasn't perfect, but it's good enough to use and heat the water.
ANALYST: It seems some hope is born … Let's stop there for today.

DR FERRO: The comments I am going to make won't really be about the sessions, but rather about the presentation of the case.

The first thing that took my attention was that the patient is in his first year at university, studying Mechanical Engineering. Although an external fact, I regard it as relevant to the analysis.

It is interesting that the analyst immediately has a reverie about him: the image of the plant ripped out of the ground, with its roots visible and needing to be transplanted elsewhere. I think that this reverie is the connecting thread in the analysis, as if she had immediately been able to have a dream about the patient's emotional situation. On the one hand, we have mechanical engineering, and on the other, the plant with the roots, with life.

One might see the need to make repairs as a reparative fantasy that is probably connected to aggressive fantasies. But I prefer to think of it in a completely different way: this "plant" constantly needs to signal to the others what type of terrain it needs in order to develop. His drama is that he cannot find an adequate place to put down roots and to grow. So in the first sessions, he adjusts the window: he repairs the analyst to make him fit for purpose.

The analyst, when he thinks of the figure of Frankenstein's monster, follows the same thread. As you perhaps remember, Mary Shelley, the author of *Frankenstein*, led a terrible life, with many bereavements and catastrophes, as well as the great problem of having been rejected by her mother. Frankenstein's monster is in some ways the other part: the plant is as desperate as he is, who then becomes violent and aggressive. His great drama is that he has been rejected by his creator, and when he feels this rejection he becomes violent.

Then begins the caterwauling, which seems to be a kind of first emotional communication, a search for affection, as if some roots of the plant had started to find a place on the couch.

Later, the analyst tells us that the patient's overwhelming feeling is one of abandonment, the feeling of someone who has neither a father nor a mother.

I am not particularly fond of the transgenerational discourse, but in this case the fact that this young man was born shortly after the parents had lost a child is relevant: it is as if we had a father and a mother who were not able to work through their grief at the loss of their child, and so he, at birth, does not find an authentically available emotional atmosphere where he can put down roots. Therefore, this defence mechanism is a way of anaesthetizing himself in the face of this drama. I see this as the leitmotiv of the story. There are great changes in the patient's way of being between the first and the second session, a year later. Now I would like to hear what you think.

AUDIENCE: In the first session, what stood out for me was the attempt by the analyst to bring the patient closer to the language of emotions. In part he accepts this invitation; in part, however, he sticks to his position, without being absolutely sure that the invitation is aimed at him. For this reason, what is striking is that the second session sees a modification and an emotional atmosphere that offers the chance to live emotions. In the first there're more mechanics; in the second more emotions.

DR FERRO: I agree that the distinguishing quality between the two sessions lies precisely in this: the first is mechanical engineering; in the second, a great emotional richness has been set in motion.

AUDIENCE: I have noticed that you, Dr Ferro, started your comments with the data given in the introduction, and not with the sessions. I would like to know why you did that, and what methodological principle lies behind this approach.

DR FERRO: We must always look for the waking dream thought. There are the dreams we have at night when we are asleep, and then there is also the constant activity of forming waking dream thought. We have to stay in contact with this waking dream thought, both the patient's and the analyst's. When an analyst makes a summary of a case, these facts can be seen as belonging to external reality, and this does not interest me. But we can also see this material as the dream that, over the course of years of work, the analyst has of the patient, especially in the way in which he transmits this information. The presentation represents a summary of the analyst's waking dream thought about the patient. So "Mechanical Engineering", "the uprooted plant", "Frankenstein's monster" are crucial nodes, not as facts belonging to the patient's external story, but because the analyst selects them and communicates them.

We can also regard the patient's reply to the analyst's intervention not as something that is connected to external reality or to his inner world, but as the dream that the patient has at that moment in response to the analyst's interpretation. If he says: "my father saw me and stayed to talk with the driver", in reply to what we might regard as an excellent interpretation, the patient, through his waking dream thought, tells us that he experienced the analyst as someone who had come closer, but then started to speak about something else. For me it is important to find the way to communicate with the patient, to discover on the basis of his reply how to talk to him, in order to understand and be understood, forgetting theory and learning how the patient perceives us through his waking dream thought. And, at times, it is necessary to transform our way of being rather than to interpret how he perceives us, so that the patient feels us closer.

The problem with this session is the problem of separation. The only way the patient can tolerate it is to make it lighter, because, if he actually does come into contact with this intensity, he cannot put up with it. He says: "No, it's not a cut, it's just an interruption". But were he able to tell the truth, he would say: "What do you expect me to do? Do you want me to tie you up with a chain and put a ball on your foot?". This is what he would like to do, but he says: "What's the point of you letting me do what I want to do if there is then no solution? It is better for me to defend myself and say: it is only an interruption". At this moment, the patient experiences the therapy as a kind of insurance policy, whereby the father pays for the car, but he has to pay for the radio and the stereo (the voice of the analyst), and he needs to be able to tone down his emotions in order to be able to tolerate it. The relationship needs to be superficial; it is as if it were made up of electrical wires that can only handle ten volts, and anything more than that will burn them through.

When the analyst comes closer and says: "If you pay in advance, as you want to, then that works as an insurance policy: you are sure of a return, what is heavy seems light", he replies: "that's an interesting idea". The patient's five minutes of silence after this interpretation seem to me to be the moment when the patient dreams, and the reply he gives — "When my father arrived, I was in the garage with the driver" — shows that he experiences the analyst's intervention as analogous to the arrival of a father, who then disappears, but after there has been a moment of contact. I would thus regard the session as a continuous oneiric narrative of the session itself.

Perhaps you remember the beautiful drawing by Escher entitled *Relativity*, where there are various stairways and one doesn't know where they are going. On one stairway we have the communications of the patient about the facts of his life: these stairs do in fact exist. Then there is another stairway, which is the patient's internal world, his unconscious fantasies. The stairs that interest us most, as analysts, are the stairway of the continuous narrative of the patient's and the analyst's waking dream thought. We can look at the session by paying attention all the time to the patient's waking dream reply after each interpretation.

When the analyst says, for example: "You understand that the heavy feelings don't go away, and perhaps you want to talk about them, get angry, argue, feel emotions", these words are designed to deepen the relationship. But when the patient recounts that he insisted that his girlfriend phone his father's wife, and she didn't want to because she thought they didn't like her, it is as if he were signalling that he experienced the analyst's interpretations as persecutory, of the type, "You don't like me". Not because they are not true, but because they are not sufficiently in tune with what the patient can bear to feel. I recall a patient who, after an interpretation I thought to be true, said to me: "Today, in A&E, I saw a child who had swallowed some nails". We cannot know what our interpretations are like for the patient before he tells us.

Here, one could start a long discussion about waking dream and narrative derivatives of $\alpha$ elements, which is what I hope to do in the first thematic seminar.

I would now like to see how the characters of the session enter into it and are transformed; for example, when the analyst says: "There are things in life that are not positive", this is not a particularly meaningful interpretation. The previous interpretation, about oppressive feelings and the possibility of anger, complaints and everything else, is much richer. But after this interpretation, the patient speaks of someone (his girlfriend) who feels certain she is not loved, while in the less meaningful interpretation, he feels that the analyst is closer to him. Indeed, after this interpretation, the mother comes on the scene. "I must go and see my mother; I haven't spoken to her for a long time". At some point, there is even mention of a phone call from his old nanny. It is as if he were telling us that this simple intervention that anyone could have given to a child, a brother, was like the nanny talking.

There's another important problem here. For me, Bion's most inexhaustible text is *Learning from Experience.* The last chapters are about the apparatus for thinking thoughts. Bion says that when a thought exceeds the capacity of the apparatus to contain it, it is evacuated, as if it were a $\beta$ element. Therefore, if the analyst's interpretation exceeds the containing capacity of the patient's apparatus for thinking thoughts — even if the interpretation is very well thought out and metabolized, rich in α elements — it generates a sense of persecution and is evacuated as a β element. The most important thing for the patient is not that the analyst finds a truth to communicate to him, or comes up with a profound interpretation, but that he is in unison with him.

AUDIENCE: I've been trying to understand the material contained in the sessions in a more global manner, taking all the interpretations highlighted by Dr Ferro as a path which might lead the patient to speak of the mother in hospital. From this point of view, both the analyst's interpretations seem to me to be part of a whole in movement.

AUDIENCE: Here in our Society, we use the term "formulation" for a communication that does not have all the prerequisites of what we call an interpretation. We do this because, if we take account of the theory of transformations, we cannot take an interpretation in isolation and say whether it is profound or superficial.

AUDIENCE: Given that the patient is a mechanical engineer, he needs an analyst who dreams, but at the same time there is a technical problem. There is a moment when the dreaming analyst must be introjected so that the engineer can also dream, otherwise the analysis is repetitive with regard to the split-off aspects. One carries on being a mechanic and the other carries on dreaming.

AUDIENCE: Looking at all the material, I felt that there was always an enormous distance between the analyst and the patient. Perhaps she managed to grasp certain aspects of the patient, but when she interpreted and when she thought, it was all very theoretical, even literary. He always brings her material that speaks to the lack of communication, to distance (the distant father, the distant mother, the distant stepmother, his difficulty in uniting with his girlfriend). In other words, he speaks of the difficulty of making contact, of coming closer to other people. In my view, the interpretations, however correct they may be, were too theoretical, lacking emotion. Perhaps there was affect inside the analyst, but I do not think that it was present in the communication.

Then at the end of the second session, there is an atmosphere of sadness that contaminates both of them. The analyst says: "At the moment you are feeling sad". There is a silence lasting some minutes, and her interpretation talks of a certain dejection, a certain sadness, when he says that he is thinking of an electrical system where the wires are cut. At this moment, I find that there is emotion; he feels concern and sadness, perhaps he feels the analyst's interest in him. And he says: "I feel like connecting the wires"; a message of hope. He finishes with: "I thought of my uncle's boiler. It was complicated, the house was old, the conductors old. In the end I managed to repair it; it wasn't perfect, but it's good enough for heating the water". At this moment, I felt that he came closer, felt his analyst closer; he warmed up.

DR FERRO: I think that the patient's drama necessarily enters into the session. And if the analyst is a good container for the patient's projective identifications, at first she will inevitably function like the insufficient mother the patient had. She must, in some way, take inside herself the patient's soil, which is made up of sand and stones, and transform it into fertile ground. In this way, the patient can at last experience a new mother, once the sand and the stones have been transformed.

Before finishing, I would like to point to what I see as the most significant moments of this transformation. One of these is when the analyst says: "I think you are afraid of dying, of hunger when you are alone, and you think that food is always outside you". Here, we have a mother of stone and sand. And the patient replies that it is not like that, that he really doesn't like being alone. Then the analyst says: "You have the idea that life is movement which is always in others, outside you. Perhaps you imagine that there is no movement inside you, just like the congestion you had to cope with this morning". Here, we have the mother of the fertile soil. And the patient replies to the mother of the fertile soil: "I have to adjust the main door to allow the car to get in". In other words: "I must open the main door to allow something you are talking to me about to come in". When the analyst says that the door can be opened from the inside out, and that this indicates that inside there is movement, congestion, but also an opening, again we have the fertile analyst. The patient's oneiric reply was: "the good thing about moving house (the house move is like saying the analyst must change) was that they started to appreciate me". Then the mother of stone and sand returns and says: "The closed door prevents entry into some unknown spaces etc."; an interpretation which the patient cannot understand.

At this moment, the patient says: "I never liked being alone". Once again he is alone. There is no longer the mother, she has disappeared, and he goes to the grandmother's bed. I think that the grandmother is the analyst from some minutes earlier, whom he had perceived as warm and close.

There's a nice conclusion: "old house, old conductors etc.... In the end I managed to repair it; it wasn't perfect, but it is good enough for heating the water". There is hope that the analyst will be transformed, and will be able to give the patient a different internal mother.

Our patients help us a lot if we are capable of hearing what they say, and if we don't interpret everything in terms of resistance, persecution, attachment etc. As analysts we do not think enough of the side effects of our interpretations. These side effects are frequently called negative therapeutic reaction, psychotic transference etc. We must learn to speak with the patient in such a way as to give him the greatest number of growth factors and the smallest number of side effects.

# Clinical Seminar III

ANALYST IN SUPERVISION: Marcos started analysis in August 1995, at the age of five years and ten months. He is now seven years old. His parents had been told that Marcos was not keeping up with the other children in the class. At times the teacher doubted whether he understood basic concepts such as "in front of" and "behind", when he had to line up with the other children. He didn't even make any drawings, just scribbles. Occasionally, he would say things that belonged to the world of his imagination but that he seemed to think were real. Also, the parents noted that Marcos expressed ideas coming from his fantasy world, out of context. They also reported nocturnal bedwetting and immaturity, "as if he wanted to stay a baby".

He is the second child and has a brother just over a year older who is seen as very lively, intelligent, and who stands out in comparison to Marcos. The father is an engineer and apparently quite a rational man. He says he is very strict and, in his own words, when he gives a command he sticks to it. He gives the impression of being affectionate and interested in the children. The mother appears uncertain and frightened of what might happen to the children, but she is capable of responding to requests for help. She shows fragility and defines herself as lacking aggression. She doesn't know how to defend herself. At one of our meetings, she said: "If someone gives me rotten tomatoes at the market, I just take them".

Marcos is a docile, receptive child, who tends to do as he is told automatically. My first impression is that he is somewhat strange, perhaps in the way he moves and the way he mixes up his words when he speaks. He used the playing materials in an impulsive and disorderly way: he would start by scribbling on one sheet of paper and end up scribbling over everything. At the first interview he said he was "born in a castle in England, but that his mother didn't know". When I asked him to tell me a story using some drawings (the CAT test), he would usually only give descriptions. In one such description he said: "There's a plush bunny in the cradle, but I … I have terrible nightmares". I found this communication very striking, akin to a request for help, and it made me think that he could not project his terrors outside himself.

At the beginning of the analysis he mostly used materials such as clay and paints. Everything spread and ran everywhere. One day the idea of a shield came out. We made lots of shields, which Marcos then took home. We made some attempts at making armour that would cover him up completely. It seemed that he was looking for a rigid container, one just for him.

Another significant moment was when Marcos started to spread plastic veneer over the palms of his hands and then took off the film of plastic that formed, slowly and patiently, piece by piece. This experiment was repeated many times; it was something he really wanted to do. He started to become more comfortable, he threw himself on the couch to make himself at home; it became possible to have a conversation with him. I had the strong impression that he was uncovering himself. I also thought of the idea of the formation of a psychical skin. During this period he asked me for a broomstick and a stick, again very significant things.

Dr Ferro: I would like make some reflections, as I think the way in which the material has been presented already shows some main themes. One emerging theme is that this child seems disorientated vis-à-vis the world of the emotions. Another theme is bed-wetting; an insufficient introjection of the containing function. It seems that there is a possibility of holding in but then a lack of control intervenes and things escape. It seems to me that he has difficulty metabolizing deeper emotions, especially in relation to aggressiveness. If the mother is offered rotten tomatoes at the market, she pays up and takes them home. The father seems to be a rational and very rigid person.

Through the game of analysis the child tells the story of the emotions that cannot be kept in. He begins with smearing material, spreading paint over the table, and ends up scribbling all over everything — like a kind of enuresis. He doesn't keep things within the confines of the sheet of paper; the container is insufficient and they get out.

The first strong communication is when he says: "There is a plush bunny in the cradle". This seems to correspond to the child the mother wanted; a calm child-bunny in a world of soft toys. But in the first communication the child talks about being born in a castle in England, and that the mother doesn't know about it, and rabbits are not born in castles in England. Perhaps knights are born in castles in England. I'm thinking of King Arthur and the Knights of the Round Table, and also of ghosts.

The child says: "There is a plush bunny in the cradle, but I have horrible nightmares, and the horrible nightmares are those that exist in castles in England". I think it is true what our colleague said: he could not project his terrors outside himself because he has always been thought of as a soft toy child-bunny, and not as a child born in a castle in England.

After this first phase, in which everything spreads beyond the confines of the page, there is a second phase in which it seems to me that, more than a container, there is a claustrum, understood as something rigid, as something that keeps in very intense, very destructive emotions. In my fantasy, then, I highlight the phrase: "We tried to make shields, armour". The armour fits in with the knights of the English castles, but has nothing to do with the quiet toy rabbit in the cradle. They suggest something very disturbing, something highly impetuous.

Then this attempt to construct a container through the skin continues. I am reminded of Bick's beautiful descriptions of the second skin, the absence of the first skin, or also of character conduits as a second skin, like the claustrum.

Another important moment is when he asks for a broomstick, a stick. If we wanted to be Meltzerian, we might think of zone confusion: in front, behind, rear end, penis and the whole dialectic between submission and aggressiveness; perfectly sensible thoughts. However, I prefer to think, for this child, of a new story which could be a previously unthought-of container. I think of what we said about the castle in England, about the armour and the stick. The stick could be seen as a kind of club, like the stick used by the knights of old when they fought in tournaments. The title could be: "A bunny for Ivanhoe".

These are my fantasies about the first phase: it is as if we now had to find room for the story of Ivanhoe. That which is evacuated in the enuresis is Ivanhoe, who must always be eliminated because there is as yet no place to contain him.

I would see Ivanhoe as being like a dream we now have about this child. This is a different way of thinking, which is not looking for a model to fit the child into, as there are many other models available. Meltzer's model would be the nearest to hand, but then there is also Bick's model or Klein's.

I think it is important that with every patient the analyst should form $\alpha$ elements for the first time, with him and for him. In this story, in which we have a rabbit in the cradle with horrible nightmares, a child born in a castle in England, armour, fear of aggressiveness on the part of the mother, and the opportunity after some analysis to make a stick, the dream that came to me is that of Ivanhoe. But there are a hundred other dreams I could have had. The important thing is to accept not only a tender and delicate part, but also a violent part in the sense of violent emotions that have not had the chance to be sufficiently thought, and which are continually evacuated — but which then, through analysis, one can start thinking about.

AUDIENCE: I was wondering whether the analyst's communication might not have been, "My mother manages to see me only as a bunny rabbit; she cannot understand that I have all these other feelings".

DR FERRO: I am calling all these other feelings Ivanhoe feelings. I agree: the mother of this child was only able to see the rabbit sleeping in the cradle and not the gorilla. Another story could have been about a gorilla.

ANALYST IN SUPERVISION: The mother said "If they give me rotten tomatoes at the market, I take them", at a meeting I had with her after I had described the child to her. She was very surprised by what I said.

DR FERRO: What did you say to her?

ANALYST IN SUPERVISION: I said that he was afraid of living his own aggressiveness; that he always tried to be careful.

DR FERRO: Here, another enormous problem arises: how to see the patient's replies, or those of a parent, *after* we have made our communication. I think we should regard them as a narrative derivative of the dream which, at that moment, the person who is conversing with us (the patient or the parents) has about the relational situation at that moment. There is a fundamental concept of Bion's, which is not related to the dreams we have at night when we sleep, but to waking dream thought: the activity of dreaming in real time. All the emotions, the sensory and emotional impressions we have at that moment and that we make into an $\alpha$ element, which is basically a visual image of which we have no immediate knowledge, but whose narrative derivatives we are able to know. This point is interesting because, at the moment when the analyst talks to the mother about aggressiveness and the child's need to be careful (she is not talking in terms of the bunny rabbit), the visual synopsis, the $\alpha$ element that the mother constructs from this situation, is the rotten tomatoes. "You are telling me that my son is a rotten tomato!". This shows us the necessity she has to see her son as a nice bunny, because otherwise he would be a rotten tomato.

In the meantime, the mother buys the goods but is not convinced. She listens to what the analyst says but maintains: "No, my son is not like that!". She pretends to take the tomatoes but without being convinced.

AUDIENCE: What do you think a Kleinian would *not* do?

DR FERRO: That's the million dollar question. I think a Kleinian would not try to construct a new story, but would be tempted to interpret aspects relative to aggressiveness, incontinence and violence immediately, without giving sufficient thought to the question of where to put these things, whereas this other way of thinking also considers the problem of where to put these things. So the story of Ivanhoe we have invented — which could be the story of a gorilla with a bunny rabbit — becomes itself a container for these violent aspects. This is what I think, but one would have to ask a Kleinian.

AUDIENCE: When you speak of violent aspects, are you thinking of aggressiveness?

DR FERRO: Not of aggressiveness, but of proto-emotions, violent and intense emotional states which, owing to an insufficient maternal function, are experienced as if they were aggressive. There is nothing aggressive about them. The point is that the inadequate maternal function makes them appear aggressive. I do not look at these things in relation to the death instinct or aggressiveness, but as something that needs to be accepted and transformed. I see the schizoid-paranoid position not as something demonical but as akin to an oil well that can either explode or provide petrol, plastic, heating. They are two different ways of looking. I think Bion's opinion is valuable; he does not talk of the transformation of the schizoid-paranoid position into the depressive position, but of a constant oscillation which extracts raw material from the schizoid-paranoid position.

ANALYST IN SUPERVISION: At present, there are moments between Marcos and me when we play calmly and even manage to joke, which never used to happen. It would seem that Marcos feels more at his ease. At times, he tries out competitive games and is pleased when he wins. Now I'll read you the account of a session:

*Marcos arrives, opens his toy cupboard and says:*

PATIENT: Help me.
ANALYST: How do you want me to help you?
PATIENT: Take them all out!

*There are some sessions when he asks me to take everything out of the cupboard and then he chooses. I start to take things out and say:*

ANALYST: You like it when I take everything out so that you can see better what you have inside.
PATIENT: Yes, I like it.

*While I am taking things out of the cupboard, Marcos says:*

PATIENT: Do you have a piece of paper?

*I try to understand what he wants. He says that it is for writing letters, that it can be plain paper. He wants me to make the envelopes and the writing sheets. Then I have to write what he tells me to write. The letters are for his father, his mother and his brother.*

*I sit down to make the envelopes, and in the meantime, Marcos picks up a toy we have made. This toy was made with the stick, which is why I talked about it. He plays a lot with the stick and with the transformations of the stick. It is made up of two pieces of cylindrical wood joined with string; he likes it a lot. Turn it around and it becomes a weapon. It is almost like a martial art.*

*Marcos repeats a movement he made at the last session: he wraps the string around the feet of the table. At the last session he enjoyed the idea that it might be difficult for me to unravel the string. Just like the last time, I say he is wrapping it up well and that it will be difficult to untie.*

*Marcos now sits at the table where I am making what he asked me to make. He takes a piece of cardboard and cuts it up into small pieces with some scissors; the pieces fall to the floor. I observe and ask him what we are going to write. He keeps on cutting up the paper and looks sad.*

ANALYST: Would you perhaps like to tell your father, your mother and your brother that at times it is difficult being the youngest in the house?

PATIENT: Yes, that's right. Do you know how to make a house, how to draw a house? We can cut up the houses and glue them to the letters.

ANALYST: Yes, I can do that.

PATIENT: But not like the one I do, in a different way.

*I draw a house and show it to him.*

PATIENT: Yes, just like that. I want to learn how to draw this house.

ANALYST: I can help you, have a go.

*I give him some tips. He draws, but he is not satisfied with the result.*

PATIENT: I wanted it to be the same as yours.

ANALYST: Yes, it's not the same, but similar. We're different, aren't we?

*He draws another house and seems to be more satisfied.*

PATIENT: Do you know how to do some stairs?

ANALYST: What?

PATIENT: Like that. Draw some stairs.

ANALYST: You can put the stairs in the house.

PATIENT: There at X, I'll have a house at the top of a tree.

ANALYST: So we'll need some stairs.

*He draws a tree. I draw a house on top and he does the stairs. Then he adds a chimney. We talk about various houses, brick houses; we remember the story of the* Three Little Pigs. *He says:*

PATIENT: Do a brick house.

*I draw a brick house. We talk of the fact that a brick house is stronger and more solid. We also draw some other buildings. He says:*

PATIENT: Put bricks throughout the building.

ANALYST: You now want to grow and become stronger. *(And I don't know why, but I repeat what I had said before: it is hard to be the youngest.)*

*He says:* "Yes, it is" *as if he wanted to say:* "You've already said that".

*Then he interrupts me while I'm drawing the building. He does a drawing and I am supposed to guess what it is. He draws a kind of chess board.*

ANALYST: Is it a cage?

PATIENT: No.

ANALYST: Is it a prison?

PATIENT: No, I'll give you a clue: it's what you have in a game of football.

ANALYST: Ah! A net!

PATIENT: Yes! And now, what's this? *(He makes another drawing.)*

ANALYST: I don't know, it's difficult.

PATIENT: The trainers of a football player. *(He draws a ball, I draw the player), and he says:*

PATIENT: I want it to be like yours, I want to learn.

*We draw some more players. He says:*

PATIENT: Do you know how to make a fan?

ANALYST: A fan?

PATIENT: What women use to fan themselves.

*He starts making a fan, folding the paper and I imitate him. I finish my fan first and as the session is at the close, I tell him that we have to put things back again.*

*While I am putting things back in place, he continues to make the fan, and rolls it up so he can take it away with him. He takes with him two clay dolls (he calls them "ghosts") which we had made during an earlier session. (Here, I digress just to explain one thing: he has shown a certain curiosity about the age, sex etc. of my children, and I don't know for certain if it was in this session or in another that we had the following dialogue: I tell him that my children are grown up and he says that I don't look that old. Then he wants to know whether it is possible to be adult and to continue living at home.)*

DR FERRO: I want to say immediately what has come to my mind, so that I don't forget.

The first communication, before the session, is that now the child is at his ease, playing competitive games and enjoying winning. And we had these fantasies about tournaments. I like the beginning of the session where the child opens up the cupboard and says: "Help me take it all out". Not taking everything out of the cupboard, but everything that is inside him.

I think this is where the need for communication begins: these notes, these cards have to be written to communicate something. Then comes the game, the transformation of the stick, with all the meanings that had formed earlier: the martial arts, the Ninja Turtles, the club used by the medieval knights.

My impression is that, at this moment the analyst should have had the capacity to wait, to see what would come out. It is as if the question, "Would you perhaps like to tell your father, your mother and your brother that at times it is difficult being the youngest in the house?" puts a lid on things, in some way stopping the ghosts from appearing. When he replies: "Yes, that's right", he is like the mother who takes the rotten tomatoes; he can't say no because he feels no would be too aggressive, like a club or a stick.

However, he finds another path: "Do you know how to make a house?". Making a house is, in some respects, making a place where something can come in. It is as if Tarzan appeared, and there was a tree house that was reminiscent of the primitive, the forest.

The analyst repeats: "It hard being small". I wouldn't consider this an error on the part of the analyst. It is as if the analyst took inside herself the mother, capable only of seeing the little bunny, but the analyst needs to metabolize this mother into a mother that can see Tarzan, the Ninja Turtle, these deeper emotions. When the football net and the goal appear, this expresses the child's desire for a mother who is open and available to receive him. It is as if there were an agreement to find an intermediary point between the boy's primitive aspects and the mother who doesn't want to know. It is as if the medieval tournament, the violent fights, were able to find an intermediary point; namely, the football pitch where violence is ritualized and subjected to precise rules. So, not exactly Tarzan or the Ninja Turtle, but also no longer the furry bunny.

This is a wonderful conclusion in which, finally, there is room for the football player's trainers — the trainers of the kicking football player. The fan reminds me of the automatic device in a car engine that brings the temperature down when it overheats.

We cannot leave each other with this football image, but we can separate with the image of eighteenth-century women fanning themselves; a breath of fresh air on a day of intense and violent football playing.

This child constantly asks a question: what kind of person is his analyst? Is she someone who can only see bunny rabbits, or can she also see ghosts? Is she afraid of ghosts? Also, the guessing game helps him see what she guesses, like the game of scribbles which Winnicott used to play with children, but in a reversal of roles. It is as if he were saying: "What fantasies are you capable of? Do you only see bunnies, chicks, things like that, or are you capable of seeing other things? And how primitive can these things be?".

Then, I think, that there is another problem, which is related to projective identifications. Some projective identifications are like notes which communicate, and there are others that the analyst receives without realizing, as, for example, that of the mother who puts the blanket over him. Knowing how to cool down emotions is the fundamental part of the functioning of the emotional engine. We cannot always deal with the emotional lava. The cooling down function makes it possible to maintain a channel of communication. Sometimes, when we stop the car and it is stationary, if the engine is too hot, the fan keeps turning.

AUDIENCE: How do you see the toy weapon he uses to tie up the legs of the table?

DR FERRO: I think that, for the moment, it is the way in which he can express disagreement. He takes the toy that they had constructed in the previous session, and goes through the motions of wrapping up the legs of the table. We don't know exactly what this corresponds to, but we can make an interpretation that decodes the meaning or a thought that constructs a meaning, which could have something to do with separation or the use of the weapon, or with the Almodovar film *Tie Me Up*, or with many other fantasies relative to that. It could also have something to do with fantasies of hunting, when one throws a weapon at the legs of an animal of prey to capture it, or thousands of others.

I would say that this child, thanks to his analyst, has travelled a long way: starting from the furry toy he has moved to the football game, to the football player's foot, right up to the fan, and the conclusion with the clay puppets, the ghosts. A very productive path.

AUDIENCE: You describe a complete creative movement that runs up to end of the session. How important is it that this creative path has a name? How important is it to make an intervention that is more connected to this path?

ANALYST IN SUPERVISION: Just to make an observation on this point: personally, I was pleased with the interaction in the session, which was unusual for this child. Everything was very fluid: he was drawing, and basically there was a sense of closeness. I understood that the session was developing, but I was unsure about what I was saying to him. I felt I should be asking myself: "Why am I saying this?". Because it seemed that there was no need to say anything.

DR FERRO: About these worries, I imagined a projective identification in which the analyst received this figure of the mother, who can only see the bunny rabbit.

Now there is another important question; namely, how to treat the progressive movement in the session.

I don't think that there is a need, moment by moment, to interpret the transformations that happen in the session. It's like making soufflé: if you open the oven door too soon, it collapses. There is no precise recipe. One needs to feel when it is necessary or useful, to make an interpretation that makes new developments possible, or when it is better to refrain from intervening. At any rate, I would chose rather to make the most of the transformations that occur in the session, playing with the characters that emerge, and not to give decoding interpretations.

AUDIENCE: I understood that at the end of the session, the child asked whether he will be able to stay inside the house when he grows up.

DR FERRO: This is the child's central question: if the analyst takes out everything there is to take out, and if he grows, will there still be space in the mind of the analyst?

Here another problem arises: namely, how to decide to what extent the mother also needs to be helped in a situation of this type. This is always a dramatic problem, in all child analyses. Unfortunately, the situation is not always one where the parents can be adequately helped, either for objective reasons or because they are unwilling. If the mother were also helped to bring out all the other aspects of herself which have never been able to come out, there would be less fear of these aspects in the child. On the other hand, I do not think that one can insist that the child will be treated only on condition that the parents are also treated. If the parents accept, a proposal of this kind may help, as long as they do not see the proposal as something persecutory.

AUDIENCE: How would you work on the aspect of narcissism that is present?

DR FERRO: Certainly narcissism is an aspect that is present in the knights of the castle. However, it is so visible as to be the narcissism that covers an enormous fragility. I would not address this so much, in the sense that I would adapt to the game, and I would accept my role as someone who does certain things for him; at least for now, and in the immediate future.

AUDIENCE: As regards the fantasy of violence, I think it is very important that the analyst functions as a container under control.

DR FERRO: I agree. A function of modulation, which is neither negation nor the rigidity of the armour. In short, the transformation of that which could not even be thought. I see the football pitch as a positive transformation. And positive transformations can be obtained without bloodshed. It seems to me a useful compromise between various different demands.

# Clinical Seminar IV

ANALYST IN SUPERVISION: Leo has been in analysis for six years. We started with five sessions a week, later reduced to four. When Leo was three years old, his mother came to me saying that her son only interacted with her, and that his use of language was developing in a bizarre way. My diagnosis was early infantile psychosis.

At present, Leo is attending a special school, and he can read and write well. His behaviour, however, clashes with that of other children of his age: he isolates himself, talks to himself for long periods, and often repeats dialogues from films or cartoons.

At the beginning of the year he was in Los Angeles visiting some relatives. Since then he has done nothing but make cardboard mock-ups of the city, complete with buildings and streets. Gradually, he has been adding details such as street lamps, cars and prams made out of clay. Initially he staged dramas with monsters that invaded the city: extraterrestrial monsters or sea monsters; enormous creatures whose frightening steps shook the houses, and who watched the children through the window. Then he went back to modelling, which he did for the first few months of last year, making monstrous clay figures: the butterfly that eats buildings; the giant lizard and the egg it came from; as well as the *Gamera*, a giant turtle that spat fire from its mouth. These three figures appear frequently in his drawings. We are now in a phase of more dialogue: Leo at least replies to the questions I ask him, and is no longer quite so inaccessible.

I think that he hit upon Los Angeles because it is a long way away, and because it is where Disneyland and Universal Studios are located: places of extreme interest to him, who always seems to have lived more on the cinema or TV screen than inside real life.

I shall briefly describe the theme of the last few sessions.

He makes a series of catastrophic drawings. The enormous butterfly is "feeding" on the city of Los Angeles and "evacuating". (When he says "feeding", he means it is eating the city.)

He draws a tired butterfly coming out of its cocoon, a teacher with his pupils and the police watching. A petrol factory catches fire (he uses the term "factory" rather than "plant"). They are all characters from Japanese cartoons. In another drawing, the giant butterfly and the *Gamera* come face to face in the middle of the ruined city. In another, a monstrous lizard with a horn appears. In the fourth drawing, two pilots and a small girl have fallen from a plane that has exploded, but they are saved by their parachutes. The control tower was destroyed by the high-speed impact of the plane, and the *Gamera* is behind it all spitting fire at the butterfly.

When I tried to talk to him about the various terrible disasters that happened in his city, he told me to "stop talking nonsense". It is important to observe that these catastrophic drawings have been a constant for years, and as much as I try to respect his need to get away from a place full of such dangers, only by trying to indicate to him how terrible it must be to live in a place like that, without pointing out that he actually does live in such a place, we seem unable to bring about any real change. My impression is that he omnipotently recreates reality through his drawings, and that this component of omnipotent recreation is stronger than his desire to share with me such experiences of destruction and horror.

Now, I shall describe a session that took place in October 1996.

*As he comes in, he asks for a piece of paper and starts to draw.*

*Figure 1*

PATIENT: This is Gnuri.

*He speaks spontaneously. Gnuri is this anima, but he doesn't explain what Gnuri is, he doesn't go into any detail. Probably it comes from some Japanese cartoon.*

ANALYST: And who's this?
PATIENT: The man … the man from the plane that has exploded. What a mess! *(He sighs.)*

*Showing signs of dejection and weariness is something new, so I decide to point it out.*

ANALYST: You're tired of so much confusion and destruction, aren't you?
PATIENT: Yes.

*At this point I ask myself if he might not have some idea, however embryonic, of the possibility that we as a pair can modify this situation.*

ANALYST: Do you think it might be possible to sort things out a bit?
PATIENT: What?

*He says this with an expression of complete absent-mindedness, as if he came from another planet; he is completely uninterested and he seems to think it absurd that anyone should ask him anything.*

PATIENT: Oh! The return … *(He takes the sheet of paper with the drawing of the* Gnuri *and emits some cries that sound like wild, prehistoric birds. Then he makes another drawing.)*

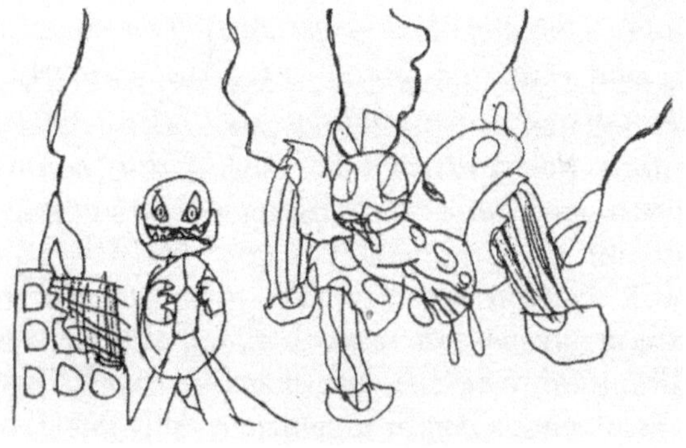

*Figure 2*

Patient: Ugh, how disgusting!
Analyst: What's so disgusting?
Patient: *Gamera*'s fire has melted the butterfly's wing. The policeman said – how horrible!

*He goes on to make another drawing that depicts the lizard's egg with the horn visible (the lizard has a horn) and the* Gamera *next to it.*

*Figure 3*

*He looks at me and says, hesitatingly, like someone looking for the right words to communicate an important fact:*

Patient: The *Gamera* has transformed into a child, into a girl …

*I need to understand who this* Gamera *is who has transformed into a girl, and to understand her function in our story.*

Analyst: Maybe she's come to bring order into the confusion?
Patient: No.

*Then he gets up from the table and moves away from me. He goes up to the couch, sits down and emits the raucous cry of the butterfly, saying that it comes from the butterfly and it is a raucous cry. Then he lies down and says with a smile, with another expression on his face: "tired". The expression on his face is half pretend — not completely, but also not very genuine. Since I find it difficult to keep up our conversation (or possibly my attention) without some closeness, I sit down next to him. He looks at me entranced, and starts tugging on a lock of my hair. It seems that this coming closer changes the nature of our relationship, which becomes more "sensual". The opportunity is there to go back to a conversation or to remain in the sphere of sensuality, if I don't pay attention. Then he puts my hair band on his head, takes it off and gives it back to me, starting a game that he enjoys a lot, and which involves imagining that he gives me things: ice cream, biscuits. But these things in reality have gone bad; in other words, they have the taste of excrement, the taste of a lizard ... And I have to show my disgust, pretending to spit. Generally, in this game, he plays the part of the analyst, taking my glasses for a moment, putting on my hair band; he is transformed into the analyst and I become Leo. But this time he is himself and I am myself. In the middle of the game, which is something of a ritual, he stops and goes back to touching my hair, in a trance.*

ANALYST: Now, you want a *Mara-seta* that is very soft, don't you? *(I use this expression because he likes soft materials and when I wear some soft fabric he strokes it and asks if it is silk; i.e. "seta".)*

*This comment has the effect of waking him up. We start playing again. But after a while I decide to talk, since I know that we could spend hours inside the same story and there seems to me to be no ludic point to this ritual; it is more like an obligation.*

ANALYST: I don't want any more things that have gone bad.

*He gets off the couch and goes over to the table.*

ANALYST: You really got annoyed when I didn't obey, didn't you?

*He makes a surprisingly wild scowl, gnashing his teeth, which he thinks are like those of a lizard. Then he makes another drawing.*

*Figure 4*

PATIENT *(He speaks spontaneously.)*: It's the bottom of the sea ... no! ... it's the beach. At night. *(He appears to be a little dejected and looks quickly to either side. The* Gamera *is pulling the lizard with the web.)*

*Later, still disheartened and with a crestfallen look, he leaves the room saying that he is going to the toilet. But he doesn't come back: he goes into another room and hides behind the furniture. I go and look for him. I want to know what frightened him so much. I imagine it was the web, the night and what I might have been transformed into. But I decide to ask him a simple, direct question.*

ANALYST: Were you afraid of me?
PATIENT *(still under the chair, laughing)*: Cosmo, you are Cosmo, the Greek.

*I don't know what he is referring to; perhaps a figure from Greek mythology.*

ANALYST: Who is Cosmo?
PATIENT: The butterfly.

*Imitating the voice of a small girl, he says "mummy" and then asks me:*

PATIENT: Mara, imitate Mara crying. *(He wants me to imitate a crying child.)*
ANALYST: I should understand children who are scared, shouldn't I?

*We go back to the room and he does the last drawing.*

*Figure 5*

*The lizard and an airplane he is controlling. He speaks this way:* The Lizard and an airplane he is controlling. *(He has a speech defect; this is typical of the kind of sentence he constructs.)*

*I tell him the time is up and he breathes a sigh of genuine relief.*

*I think that this, in fact, is my comment, because the session has been full of intense emotions. He is unable to formulate them clearly unless expressed in cries and scowls. All this has been catalyzed by our being together.*

ANALYST: It's nice to be able to forget all these dangers, isn't it?

*I am uncertain about many things, but there is one question in particular I would like to address: should I regard the patient as my best colleague, as I do with Leo, who seems to work decidedly against the perception of reality, and sometimes against the possibility of establishing contact between us? The sequence of the later sessions, and of all these years, shows once again that the drawings and the models crystallize a situation of panic, where his intention is to distort and control reality omnipotently, which also includes cancelling out my living presence, even completely at times.*

DR FERRO: Let's carry on with yesterday's seminar by talking of the analyst's dream. I shall try to construct an overall view and also point out some technical problems.

I would like to use my feeling of great disorientation, caused by the fact that I don't exactly understand which animals we are dealing with (I haven't understood what this *Gamera* is, whether it's a tortoise or an insect). It almost seems to correspond to this child's great disorientation vis-à-vis his violent emotional turbulence, which is triggered in him by the slightest contact, as if a set of proto-emotions were activated. This is reminiscent of the film *Jurassic Park*. It is as if this set of emotions were so violent, terrifying and incomprehensible that he doesn't know where it comes from and where it's going. It is as if here we could properly see the concept of emotional turbulence: something that is activated like a hurricane or a waterspout.

I think that what this child acquires is the ability to dream and to give some form of representation to these intense and violent emotions, which he then calls tortoise, butterfly — animals that move like those of prehistoric times.

This comes before the relationship that may be constructed with the analyst. It is as if the encounter between analyst and patient had unleashed a violent wind, a whirlwind, as if during our encounter a hurricane came and sent all the objects in the room flying: the microphone, the water jug, the chairs, everything. And at moments like these there is no situation to describe, because everything is in senseless movement. We can only hope that the storm abates, and then we might be able to describe in detail what has happened.

There is a wonderful book by an Austrian author, Robert Schneider.[1] It describes the experience of a boy who has a

1 Schneider, R. 1995. *Brother of Sleep*. New York: Overlook Press.

heightened awareness of every single sound: if an ant runs in the garden, he hears its steps like a terrible racket; when it is hot and he sweats, the noise made by the evaporating sweat is infernal. The book describes all the violence that overwhelms us, which we can do nothing about in this world of subliminal noises of which we are normally unaware. For this reason, I think what happens between the analyst and the patient is already an invaluable solution: they manage to contain the situation within the borders of those sheets of paper.

I also appreciated the delicacy with which the analyst makes minimal interventions, careful not to provoke emotional turbulence beyond what already exists. But on more than one occasion my impression is that, when these minimal interventions refer to the relationship, they cause the reappearance of violent electrical discharges. I want to point out some of the places where this happens.

I think Los Angeles is a good choice, both because it is far away and because it is the site of Disneyland. This means that it contains the hope of being an area of play, a kind of transitional area. And there is also a play on words: Los Angeles as "the angels". Here we are dealing with demons, but there is also the opposition between angels and demons. The world of cartoons is the right setting for this two-dimensional representation, which seems to be the sole form of survival in a world of such violent emotions.

I want to point to some sections which I think are particularly important. Technically speaking, what I am about to say may constitute a breach of the rules. I am talking about the beginning of the session when the child starts doing his first drawing. At a certain point, the analyst says: "That's right. You are tired because of all this confusion and destruction". And the analyst thinks: "I want to see whether there might be even the germ of an idea, whereby the two of us as a couple might be able to deal with this serious situation".

She makes an interpretation that, if given to any other patient, would be calm, adequate and especially useful, and might help the patient construct some meaning. She says: "Do you think we have any chance of organizing all of this?" I would like to discuss with you the patient's reply to this intervention. The patient says: "What?" and then, "Oh! The return". He takes the drawing and begins to make noises like a wild, prehistoric bird.

This reply informs us about the way in which the patient's waking dream thought has received the interpretation; in other words, what might appear to be a gentle interpretation is like the cry of wild, prehistoric birds for this child. The session proceeds and he says that the *Gamera*'s fire burnt the wings of the butterfly, as if a relational contact, even when it is delicate, was experienced as a fire that burns up the possibility of thought. From the technical point of view, much courage is required to do without any possible interpretations that might regard all that as violent and destructive aspects of the child. But this child would have no place to put such an interpretation.

I am referring to content interpretations which would take these birds and prehistoric creatures and interpret them as if they belonged to the child. We are in the presence of an $\alpha$ function of the patient that is so diminished that any stimulus, however minimal, provokes tragic emotional effects. I am reminded of what I said in the previous seminar[2] in relation to the apparatus for thinking thoughts. According to Bion, if this apparatus is stimulated by a thought that exceeds its capacity to contain the thought, the latter is evacuated as if it were a $\beta$ element, and the patient feels a great sense of persecution. Technically, it would be necessary to find a way to make small steps towards this patient, momentarily giving up even minimal interpretations of relational contents, so as to allow for the development of a story about the terrible things that happen.

If you observe other parts of the session, every time the analyst makes adequate interventions, such as: "The *Gamera* came here to put order in the confusion", the patient says, "No", gets up, moves away and emits the wild sound of the butterfly. After this emotional turbulence, which releases the violent tensions set in motion by the encounter, there is a very nice moment when there is some contact, which is when they start to play a game.

Even while playing, when the analyst gives a more direct interpretation of the relationship — for example, when he says: "You're annoyed with me because I didn't obey you" — the patient responds with a wild grimace, saying that he is a lizard. He makes the drawing in which the *Gamera* drags the lizard with the web, as if the words of the analyst for him were like a dangerous

2 See Thematic Seminar I.

spider's web. When the emotional turbulence abates, there are moments of intense communication.

I would like to stop here and listen to your opinions as to how we situate ourselves vis-à-vis this patient, in a similar way to someone who operates like an $\alpha$ function, without interpreting what is done. I am thinking especially of certain brilliant passages in Bion's *Learning from Experience*,[3] where he describes the development of the container. He says that the development of the container occurs through the formation of emotional threads that form a web, inside which — if the analyst has sufficient negative capability to tolerate doubt and waiting — at a certain moment the development of the container will also occur, without the need for interpretation. Content, therefore, is something that takes form and develops when emotional threads are created between patient and analyst which join them together, often without any interpretation being necessary.

So, faced with this child I would behave as if he were my best colleague; the best colleague inside one of those extremely violent Japanese cartoons. In other words, we would be two colleagues, two directors who, for the moment, are occupied only with the construction of this story. If a love affair then starts between these two directors, this will be the emotional affair that develops between the two. But meanwhile, we are still in the prehistoric period.

Now, I would like to hear what you have to say.

AUDIENCE: What type of connection could there be between this way of behaving and the state of primary maternal concern?

ANALYST IN SUPERVISION: I'd like to ask a question about a major uncertainty of mine. However much I might want to consider him a colleague who will construct a certain story together with me, it seems to me that it is very difficult for him to take on this role. He seems to resist participating with me in any construction which is not in the form of drawings, and all I can do is make a few comments about them. So, I would like to know how to work against this current.

AUDIENCE: Emotional turbulence was present here too, because we were a little confused as well. I have the impression that the patient's turbulence is expressed in the atmosphere and the content

3 Bion, W. R. 1962. *Learning from Experience*. London: Heinemann.

of the drawings. It seems to me that from a formal point of view, the patient achieves a better use of the α function in his drawings, because the lines he draws are resolute, firm, objective. Also, the use of space is intelligent; a formal balance is constantly upheld. So, since he seems to have the sensory, formal aspect under control, could that not be a starting point for possible communication?

AUDIENCE: In the context of the session, what would you say about the patient touching the analyst's hair?

DR FERRO: The first question is not easy. The relationship between negative capability and primary maternal concern takes us back to Winnicott. He is a writer I am very fond of, who I regard as very Bionian — or perhaps it is Bion who is very Winnicottian. Winnicott's book on scribbling is, in my view, the first to talk about a field involving analyst and patient where both participate equally.

I would pose the question about primary maternal concern as follows: what would a mother do if she realized that every time she gave her child certain food it had terrible diarrhoea? The mother's concern in this case would be to find ways of providing food, and getting the dosage right. There is a wonderful book, *La Douleur* by Marguerite Duras (literal translation: "*suffering*"; English title: *War: A Memoir*), where she describes what happens when a concentration camp survivor starts taking food again. He is given a minute quantity of meat extract on the tip of a teaspoon, and this small amount of food causes him extreme pain, vomiting and diarrhoea, because his stomach had completely collapsed, and he is no longer able to digest food. In this book there is, in my view, an extraordinary description, which goes on for several pages, of how this miniscule quantity is administered, in progressively larger doses. Then, after many pages describing the catastrophic effect of this food, the man starts to eat again.

The analyst's doubt, expressed in the second question, about how to establish a pact with the patient, reminded me of a small child who made drawings for me based on the story of *Beauty and the Beast* and, at some point, she said that I was not supposed to play the part of Beauty or the Beast, but that both of us had to be the cups. So for a long time I was a cup, without any chance of interacting except as a thinking, physical presence, but every now and then I would give that tiny amount of food on the tip of a teaspoon.

As for the question of turbulence: the problem is what to do when such violent turbulences are activated. I appreciate the protracted work of the analyst because when I think about it, such emotional turbulences have taken a creative path. They could have transformed into hallucinations or become serious psychosomatic disorders. Instead, they have taken this extremely figurative and creative path. Given that much thought has gone into this, I am very confident and hopeful that, in the future, further transformations will take place.

It is not easy to give an answer to the question about touching the hair. All I can do is tell you my dream relative to this. It is as if we had two colleagues from the Walt Disney Corporation who work together, producing their *Jurassic Park* storyboard. While this happens, an emotional relationship starts up between the two, and one of the colleagues makes a pass at the other.

AUDIENCE: When you said that this child and the analyst are not yet part of history and but are still in a period of prehistory, I think you are talking about the two companions who have started to draw the *Jurassic Park* storyboard together, where the story starts from a working relationship in which an emotional relationship between the two might develop.

In this prehistory, in which the analyst enters as the companion of the hero from the Japanese cartoons — and the place where this role is worked through will necessarily be his countertransference — what type of information about the patient could the analyst gather from observing this countertransference?

AUDIENCE: I entirely agree with the idea that the patient bears witness to his difficulties with stimuli. Trying to transcribe it onto the Grid, in terms of representation, I think it would not go beyond Row C vertically, and 3 horizontally. I think that he resists any suggestion by the analyst to bring him back to a place where he can have preconceptions or concepts. When any action is suggested, he is desperate; for example, faced with the appeal to "bring order into this confusion", he runs away; when a suggestion is made, he says: "I'm tired". So my impression is that there is very little space for action between C and 3, in the corner of the Grid.

As for the patient who asked the analyst to be a cup, she clearly must have read Bion, seeing as she wanted a container.

AUDIENCE: On the subject of *Jurassic Park*, what stood out were the horrors of the drawings. But I thought of the extreme pleasure people obtain from horror and monster movies, which they watch knowing full well that it's not real. I think, then, that this is what he wants from the analyst: he wants them to live the terror of these drawings together, but so as not to go mad. It is a situation of terror, which is, however, under control, and in this sense the drawings preserve part of the child's mental health, and enable him not to succumb to hallucinations. It is his way of working through most of the situations; he intends to live through them with the analyst by his side, which will make the situations of terror more tolerable.

AUDIENCE: The analyst mentioned the patient having some language or speech disorder. What view would you take of this speech disorder of the child and the whole process of symbolization?

DR FERRO: I would take a step backwards. I would be the companion of the Japanese hero, the partner of the person who produces the Japanese animated cartoon together with me. However, the cup we mentioned must be a thinking cup, and the place for these thoughts is the countertransference of the analyst. Today we are in Row C of the Grid, but certainly in some respects, he is in Row A. There is this transformation from A to B, from B to C, as something that still needs to be worked through. For the moment he cannot go beyond C, because for the moment leaving this position would be terribly persecutory. I think that it is possible to try to go a little further along the horizontal axis, C3, C4, C5, and to pay more selective attention in this direction, while still remaining in Row C.

Row C also relates to the other question about the pleasure of drawing, which is a kind of non-dangerous transitional space. It is, however, very dangerous when something that is in the drawing leaps out and becomes a threatening three-dimensional presence in the reality of the consulting room. Here, too, it is worth keeping the metaphor of the teaspoon, but still only offering what fits on the tip of the spoon.

For the moment, I would not pose the problem of how the pathology is manifested. I would work without focusing on the pathology, confident that emotional transformations will be able to modify the symptom itself. There are moments in which preconceptions about possible transformations arise. For example, there is a moment when a terrible monster might transform into a child, into a woman. We must wait for him to acquire the capacity to transform into a bigger container, a bigger cup. However, I would not be too concerned about the quality of this symptom.

ANALYST IN SUPERVISION: I wanted to add something about the pleasure of drawing. This child started to draw a year after the beginning of the analysis, when he was four and a half, and all his drawings were extremely creative. However, in terms of development in real life, there has been virtually no progress. He behaves exactly like a psychotic child and psychotic adolescent. So the point remains: despite all the creativity and the pleasure he may experience, these drawings are not used for growth, either because I cannot help him in this respect, or because he erects very concrete and crystallized obstacles, or because of an unfortunate combination of the two.

DR FERRO: Perhaps, so that we can go away with a touch of hope, we should remember that these processes take a long time. I think that the other aspect of primary maternal concern is this negative capability of waiting, confident that things can happen. I have a patient who has been in analysis for twenty years, and now it seems that something is happening.

# Thematic Seminar II

ANALYST IN SUPERVISION: I am going to talk about a young man I shall call Bruno. He is twenty years old, tall, physically well-proportioned, likeable and good-looking. His father is Asian and his mother South American. He has two brothers, one slightly older, the other much younger. He sought analysis after an accident in which he lost his left eye: while he was surfing, he fell in the water and when he put his foot on the surfboard to get back on again, it came up and hit him straight in the face, perforating his eye. The piece of rope connecting the surfboard to his foot was too short.

After various surgical attempts to save his eye, more than once he was forced to spend anything from fifteen to twenty days in a bed face-down, completely at rest, looking downwards through a window-like opening in the bed, designed so that he could read and watch television. For a long time he was unable to sleep or to dream.

He sees his father as stiff and cold; he is someone who has kept himself separate from his children despite providing them with every material comfort. The mother, on the other hand, is perceived as very fragile, and she despairs at seeing her children in any difficulty. She cries easily and is offended if anyone confronts her with anything. All it takes is a banal comment on daily life — for example, the simple statement that someone cooks differently from her — for her to feel denigrated.

At the beginning of our work, Bruno would speak in a continuous, monotonous way, without punctuation or intonation, without putting facts or feelings in context, which set me at a distance, and meant I had difficulty in remembering the content of the sessions and what had happened during them.

His contact with his inner world seemed slight. He was very impulsive, and often lost control: he would punch walls, the fridge and, on several occasions, he had had to have his hands bandaged because he had sprained them. Other times, he would take his car and drive along streets and roads at high speed.

Later on in the analysis, he refers to the anguish that he feels in relation to photography. He says he feels under pressure to be included in any photograph taken in his vicinity. In addition, he makes extra copies of all these photos, or asks his father to do so, fearing that they might be stolen or lost. He comments on this attitude by saying: "If one of them disappears from my sight, it is as if I did not exist".

I recount here a fragment of the session that I consider crucial to his analytic process, and which relates to his ability to dream for the first time. It happened during a session that took place after about one year of analysis.

*Bruno described trying to solve a mathematical problem where he had confused the terms of the problem: he had understood R$ 1,200 plus ten instalments, instead of R$ 1,200 in ten instalments. He was upset to realize he had made a mistake and, something new for him, had gone to talk to the professor. To his surprise, the professor had taken into account his reasoning and accepted his answer to the problem. I said:*

ANALYST: The professor listened to you. He didn't follow the rules. You were heard, he took you into consideration.

PATIENT: He considered my reasoning, even though I got the terms of the problem wrong.

ANALYST: He wasn't a prisoner of the rules.

*He remained silent and after a few minutes, still during the session, fell asleep. This was the first time that had happened. When he woke up, he was quite astonished and said he had dreamt.*

PATIENT: I was on holiday on a beach. There were some people, I think they were friends of mine, and I went to a big house I didn't know. When I arrived at the house — where I had never been before — I saw a friend wearing one of my diving suits. This friend had borrowed it some time ago and now that he had run into me he told me that he wanted to give it back. I replied that I didn't care. Then he explained to me that this suit was all rubber, with long sleeves and long legs. He also said he had rubber boots that clung to the surfboard. This suit stopped water getting in, which kept the body warm. He said: "The boots are good, but they restrain movement". In the dream I was no longer interested in the suit for this reason. I said I preferred suits with short sleeves and Bermuda shorts, even though it meant you could feel the cold water.

Now I'm going to describe a recent session; the second session of the week, two years after the beginning of the analysis.

Bruno arrives, says hello, lies down and starts to speak.

PATIENT: I've just been doing some group work at the university. I've been working very hard and it's made me tense. Yesterday, I had to work hard on this task and had to take care not to make mistakes. There were lots of cards; big cards with lots of numbers.

*He gesticulates while he speaks, making movements as if he could still see the material he was working with earlier.*

PATIENT: This time P. and M. *(two colleagues)* were working with me. We worked non-stop until 7 p.m. *(He emphasizes this point.)* I had already done other work for the faculty and again I had to pay a lot of attention so as not to make mistakes. I was dead tired, and later, I was supposed to go swimming. But I was so tired that I thought I'd give it a miss. But S. *(his girlfriend)* insisted that I went. I wasn't sure, but I told her I wasn't coming. I ended up leaving S. at the swimming pool and then I went home. I wasn't even a block away. However, then it occurred to me that something might happen; I didn't know what, but something might happen. I turned round and went back and went swimming. In the end, I regretted it.

*Gradually, as he spoke and gesticulated, an image formed in my mind: I told him that he conjured up in me the image of a pavement made up of symmetrical black-and-white mosaic pieces, where you have to tread carefully, to make sure you only step on one of the two colours. And he said:*

PATIENT: Wow! I've never talked about these things before because I'm ashamed. I feel like I'm half-retarded. But since you've spoken about it and I'm here to talk about what really happens to me, I've got loads of things like that. To give you an example *(he continues with an air of resignation, which betrays effort and suffering)* — and this is only the most common example — I can't cross the street at a pedestrian crossing because I can only put my foot on the white stripe, and sometimes this is difficult because there are other people crossing the street. Walking becomes complicated, but since I have the feeling that there is a difference in level between black and white, if I put my foot outside the white stripe, it gets cut off. So, sometimes — in fact, quite often — I avoid zebra crossings because I don't want to get upset.

ANALYST: You ask me if I can assess everything that disturbs you.

PATIENT: In my high school, the floor had large mosaics and it was complicated having to put my foot right in the middle: I had to jump to do it and it was very irritating. I felt ridiculous, so I didn't go out during break. I know I must have looked like a retard. I'm annoyed at myself, but it doesn't help. I think there are lots of things that might happen if I don't do what I'm supposed to do. I have to be super-careful so that nothing happens, and I'm still really afraid of appearing silly. The worst thing is that, lately, I've started to realize that almost everything is the fault of my head.

*After a few minutes' silence he goes back to the previous subject:*

PATIENT: When I went back to the swimming pool, I imagined I would find S. irritated and annoyed with me for not having stayed with her, and lots of other things even more tragic than that. Then suddenly I realized that she was fine, and totally different from the S. I expected to find. I've noticed this on other occasions. This morning, the professor took a look at the task we were doing and found it okay, without even looking at what we'd written. And that scared me.

ANALYST: You say you realized that it is something that happens inside you, which functions as a warning signal. *(I have the impression that I have acted too soon, before he has completed this movement of his. He interrupts me, as if to finish my sentence for me.)*

PATIENT: And it sees everything I do.

*He drew back and silence set in. He seemed to be thinking. In the minutes remaining before the end of the session, I remember something he said about problems to do with the homework he did at school.*

DR FERRO: I would like say I'm happy to be here and to realize how our ways of working correspond. This makes me feel so much at home that I tend to speak Italian quickly, forgetting that we need a translator.

I would like to talk about some of the associations the material suggests to me.

There is the problem of a patient who has lost his sight and is afraid of not being seen. This can be the starting point for many different stories. I felt that the loss of sight at the beginning of the story is ultimately transformed into a sentinel who looks too much. We can imagine such a thing as being "blind with rage" because there is something tied to a rope that is too short, which is then directed against the patient himself. There is the story of a boy not sufficiently watched over and cared for, who is distressed if he is not photographed, if he is not seen. I wonder if a child who is not seen by his parents ends up being watched over by an extremely persecutory superego.

So, when he has his moments of self-aggression, I would pay attention to these two movements — being blinded by rage, and blinding a persecutory superego — because it is the story of a patient who had a father and mother, but who felt they were insufficiently present. I find interesting and fascinating the story of a patient who loses control, who punches walls and refrigerators, which is not normal behaviour.

We can think of these facts as the ongoing narrative of a contact that is becoming more and more violent in reaction to the lack of a containing function. It is as if there had been no maternal or paternal mind willing to be penetrated by proto-emotions, β elements and the anguish of this boy, who continues to tell this terrible story, punching walls and refrigerators: fists against an α function, which is cold and inhospitable. There is a difference between seeing the violence of the patient as instinctual, instinctive, and seeing it as incontinence, as explosive violence caused by an insufficient metabolism. This could be the first point of reflection: it is as if there were a large quantity of as yet undigested proto-emotions which have not been welcomed or given the opportunity to be transformed.

It seems to me that from the very first words of the analysis the patient begins to write an entirely different story, together with the analyst. Already in the first fragment of the session, after the patient has spoken of his anguish at not being taken into consideration, there is a beautiful scene.

Allow me to make a short digression. I do not know if it has already been shown in Brazil, but there is a film by Ettore Scola entitled *The Family*. There is a scene in the film where a child hides and his uncle cannot find him. At some point, the child, who has hidden in a corridor, appears and the uncle, as a joke, pretends not to see him. The child is increasingly disoriented, and breaks down completely and begins to cry in despair, because he doesn't understand that his uncle is just pretending.

I think that not being seen and not being considered is one of the most intense primitive anxieties that exist: a strong, basic anguish that has to do with the conception of time, which we mentioned in another seminar.[1] It seems that, in the sessions presented here, the patient begins to discover that he can be seen — or heard (since during a session people are heard more than seen) — and is surprised to perceive the analyst's emotional willingness to accept his point of view. There was a problem formulated in a certain way and the professor, who in the session is the analyst, does not figure as an unreceptive refrigerator or a wall, but tries to accommodate the patient's point of view, and he reports that he has been heard and taken into consideration. This is the first magical moment of this encounter, in which he is being watched over, or listened to, with a benevolent eye. The patient says: "He considered my reasoning, even though I got the terms of the problem wrong". Therefore, I believe that a benevolent eye and ear are the first elements that activate any transformation.

Let me add some images that come to me at this moment. I was thinking that the point of conversion in Victor Hugo's *Les Misérables* is the moment when Jean Valjean the convict escapes from a penal colony. It is a stormy night, and he knocks on the door of the Bishop's house, where he is given food and lodgings for the night. During the night, Jean Valjean gets up, steals all the Bishop's silverware and runs away. Shortly afterwards, the police arrest Jean Valjean and bring him back before the Bishop, explaining that they had found the thief who had stolen his silverware. And the Bishop says that Jean is not a thief and that he himself had given him the silverware as a gift. This is the moment

1 See Thematic Seminar I.

when Jean Valjean changes, repents. There is a fundamental transformation in his life after this emotional experience: standing before someone who does not accuse him, but understands his point of view and his needs.

The ear or the eye of the analyst should be like those of this Bishop and not those of the sentinel or guard who looks too much. I think this story with the analyst develops along this axis: the patient describes how he feels progressively less need to defend himself. Thus, the entire session can be thought of as an impassioned narrative the patient tells about the work he does in the university analysis, where his point of view meets with confirmation, and is not denied by the analyst's interpretation. For example, after he has talked about working in the faculty with friends, about all the work he has done and how tired he is, the analyst does not interpret this as referring to the work done by him in the analysis. He lets the patient keep these treasures, the candelabra and the silver trays, without saying "They are mine". In this way, he creates an emotional climate that grants the patient freedom to narrate.

There is another fragment that made a deep impression on me. The analyst's reverie is surprising: the image of black and white appears in the analyst's head as if by magic. I don't think that all analysts would have had this image. I certainly wouldn't. But this shows us how every analysis has its own story, which depends on the mental functioning of patient and analyst.

This intervention by the analyst opens up a narrative path that is utterly transformational. I don't think that this is the only path for possible transformations. With twenty different analysts, there would be twenty different paths and twenty different stories. Here, he takes the black and white path, which connects up with tolerable and feared aspects of himself, and has to do with obsessive control over something this patient fears greatly. It may be, in equal measure, his own anger and dissatisfaction, and the persecutory eye with which his superego sees everything. On the other hand, he meets the gaze of the analyst, a look that is not at all persecutory, and, indeed, he describes finding his girlfriend different from how he imagined her: not angry, but emotionally available. Then he says: "The professor took a look at our work and found that we had done a good job. And to think that I was scared". It is as if he saw that during the analytic session his most frightening fantasies do not come to pass and his theory — that furious anger equals furious persecution — is not confirmed. Instead, he finds that there is a benevolent eye watching over the work he is doing. The analyst's communications have the quality of being very discreet. It is as if, at any moment during the session, things might happen that are different from what the patient imagined at the outset; like Jean Valjean who, when the police brought him to the Bishop, imagined having to go back to prison, but then the meeting opened up an altogether new and different story.

The analyst's gaze is what enables him to leave behind repetition compulsion and to enter the previously unthought-of area of a new story, like Jean Valjean, who adopts a child and whose story then goes on in a completely unexpected way.

So, the analyst's looking and hearing are fundamental. I always remember the words of a child, words I even once quoted in a book. He told me there was a stone which was as hard as a diamond (and he made a drawing), and that if the stone he had drawn were placed inside a bowl containing a special liquid, it would be seen that it was not a diamond but a very fragile crystal. I think that liquid represents the quality of the analyst's seeing and hearing.

My way of looking at the session is to see it as something that refers, in all the patient's narratives, to what happens inside the consulting room. I understand the concept of field differently from Willy and Madeleine Baranger. They talk about the analytic couple's unconscious fantasy, which can only be revealed with the aid of the analyst's second interpretative gaze. I see the field as the place where all possible stories can be told, stories that have their origin when the patient's undigested facts encounter the transformative ability of the analyst. It does not matter which direction this story will take later. The important thing is that it transforms the material the patient has been unable to digest, and I think that analysts with different models can perform this type of transformation equally well.

This is because, if the undigested facts are transformed, it matters little in which dialect this is done: in the dialect of the reconstruction of the child's story of events; or in the dialect of the events of the inner world, and of the vicissitudes of his internal objects; or else via a relational explanation of the here and now; or simply — which is what I prefer — by means of constant co-narrative transformations involving analyst and patient.

I do not know if, at this point, I can tell my first dream analysis … but perhaps there is no reason not to. It was my first session. I was totally unaware of how a session of psychoanalysis worked, and it seemed reasonable to me to recount a dream at my first session. So I said: "Last night I had a dream, it was a nightmare I had when I was a child … I was in my bed … I was in my cradle, and behind me there was a terrible wolf wearing glasses".

Even today, I shudder to think what the analyst might have said after this dream. And I think that if he had said that, I would not be here today. These first sentences are all I remember of my analysis; I remember nothing else. I remember the analyst saying something like this: "Clearly it must be scary being in a room with a wolf", and I remember that, at that point, there was an initial transformation of the field, because I replied to this interpretation by saying: "In actual fact, the room in the dream reminded me of a room in my aunt's house, where I used to go to learn a new language, French". After that, I remember nothing.

We can see here the root of a transformation brought about by an unsaturated interpretation, thanks to a benevolent eye that knows not to interpret everything that could be interpreted.

Getting back to what we were talking about before: I wonder whether drives and unconscious fantasies must be regarded as things in themselves, with their own strength and intensity, or whether they are somehow a function of the field that they encounter. Basically, it is the same question you could ask about violent projective identifications: is it an absolute concept, or a concept relative to the quality of the container it encounters? In today's psychoanalysis, can we still speak of drives or unconscious fantasies that belong exclusively to the patient or, conversely, are they connected to the mental qualities of the analyst? Must the unconscious fantasies and drives that enter the field be thought of as belonging to the patient, or to the analytic couple, and therefore include the analyst? Can there be a neutral analyst or does the analyst come along with their history, with their psychic life, with their drives, with their unconscious fantasies?

I'll stop here, but I'd like to hear some of your comments or replies to these questions — questions I put to myself and I'm now putting to you.

AUDIENCE: Regarding the session, you said that the behaviour of both the analyst and the bishop broke a repetition compulsion. The notion of drive seems necessary to me, to think about both repetition compulsion and the transformations that break away from it. The notion of drive also seems necessary for thinking about this demanding, assiduous superego that we try to modify in the analytic situation.

DR FERRO: I'd like to hear a few more questions and observations, and then comment on them all together. I would like at least four observations — I don't know why I say four — perhaps because of the four sessions.

AUDIENCE: Readers of your book *The Bi-Personal Field: Experiences in Child Analysis* have been charmed and enchanted,[2] but they have also been left with many doubts. My question is this: would it not be possible to complement a non-rigid structural point of view with a field theory that enables us to see the relationship? Is there necessarily an opposition between the two? The story of the here and now of a session can, metaphorically, condense many stories, in line with a philosophical idea of what psychical time is and time in psychoanalysis: a condensation of the past and a condensation of the future.

AUDIENCE: My colleague has mentioned the wealth of information to be gained by studying your book, but also the doubts it raises. One point where I had doubts was where you argue that a crucial mental attitude of the analyst, good for picking up the mental situations, would necessarily imply the absence of a referential concept, as if the use of theory contaminated the field, interfered with the possibility of conceiving the situation.

In relation to the clinical material that you have dealt with, and the question of drives in psychoanalysis today, I would like to take another approach, almost the reverse of this approach, and which I think contains the most important contributions in the area of early psychoses. Anne Alvarez has examined patients like this, who have not been looked at properly; something that generates deficit situations. But Alvarez uses the whole mass of information of developmental psychology to capture situations that might have had some potential in these psychotic children, and which have

2 Ferro, A. 1999. *The Bi-Personal Field: Experiences in Child Analysis*. London, New York: Routledge.

either never come to pass, or have led to specific types of deviations. She starts from this theoretical conceptual information, pointing out mental situations that are not directly manifest in these patients, in order to better reveal deficit situations. Approach techniques, such as the notion of a complaint starting from the notion of deficit, lead the analyst to have a more active role in trying to help these patients. Hence, I believe that the discovery of certain mental situations often depends not so much on a discovery made during the analytic session, but on an assessment of a whole set of information we get from the patient, where it may be important to distinguish what is essential from the rest. I would like to hear your opinion on this.

AUDIENCE: Talking about the clinical material, Dr Ferro said that it is as if the patient had not experienced maternal or paternal containment. Are they the same thing for you? I wanted to know something about your ideas regarding paternal containment in the structuring of the child's psyche.

DR FERRO: There are many interesting questions here. I think models are approximate narratives recounting what we think we have understood, and that any model must be regarded as provisional. Inevitably, behind each model lie the models that preceded it.

I am interested in finding new models when it seems that there may be a new, more satisfying way of narrating things. The concept of drive would help us to understand the question of repetition compulsion. But a concept that helps me more — and gives me an equal opportunity to understand repetition compulsion — is the idea, for example, that there are some facts in the patient that have not been digested; that is, accumulations of elements that keep knocking on the door until they are transformed into something different. I find I can operate better within this model.

On the other question, I think that the models can be complementary and that the analyst cannot function in a rigid way. The work done on the field, on the here and now, is inevitably carried out with a view to transforming the patient's inner world. It is possible to rewrite his history, or at least to render it partially different. In other words, we cannot give up either the Freudian or the Kleinian vertex.

As for the use of theory during the session: at times, theory can cover over the patient's material and become a kind of transformation in hallucinosis, whereby the analyst sees in the session what he injects into it from theory. But it is different with the reveries that the analyst may have during the session. I believe that the observation of babies can be an endless source of reverie, but another analyst may find it useful to consider the stages of development.

As regards the problem of the here and now: do you remember the theory of fractals in mathematics? According to this theory, the same structure is repeated constantly, on a large scale, medium scale and small scale. So, what happens in the session is, on a micrometric scale, what can happen in real life and in inner life. For me, it is enough to look under the microscope of the session, to consider all the patient's stories as related to the session, even those that seem to belong to external reality. But this does not mean "refuting" what he says. For example, if the patient tells me that when he was little his aunt used to shout in his ears, I do not interpret this as something that happens in the session. But I try to talk to him so that he does not experience me as the aunt who yelled in his ears.

As for the maternal and paternal function, I wonder why a father should not also have the pleasure of contributing to the formation of the child's α function. I believe that the α function has no gender; it is as maternal as it is paternal. It is clear that there are different maternal and paternal functions, but only at more advanced stages of development.

Let me conclude by mentioning a science-fiction story that may perhaps help us to reflect on the question of drives. It is a story by Ray Bradbury, a fascinating science-fiction writer, about a house in the future where everything is completely automated. In the morning, the children are washed and dressed by wonderful machines. Just press the button before you leave home and you will find everything ready for lunch; press other buttons and your clothes are washed, hung out to dry, ironed and put in place. There is only one place in the nursery where there is something not automated: one of the walls of this room can become three-dimensional and acquire depth. The fantastic scenes that the children are living come to life on these walls. If they read a book, the characters that occupy their minds immediately acquire life in this three-dimensional space.

At some point, the parents become concerned because they see that more and more violent scenes with wild animals, with lions and tigers devouring other animals, are coming to life on this wall. So they decide to switch off the machine that makes the wall three-dimensional. The children are desperate because, for them, this wall is the only living thing in the house. They get permission to play for the last time, before the wall is permanently shut off. Then the children call their parents into their room and the story ends with the parents watching the animals that have become real, which then come out from the wall and devour them.

We have to think of the drive as something that can be contained if there is an available reverie, and a mental depth capable of receiving it mentally. But the drive is acted out if, in contrast, this possibility of reception, containment and transformation is precluded.

Therefore, the drive, like the lion, always needs to be thought of in relation to this maternal or paternal function of the mind, to find room for it. If the maternal or paternal function is insufficient, the lion comes out in truly destructive form.

# Clinical Seminar V

Analyst in supervision: Lia came to me for analysis because she felt very fragile, empty and lifeless. She would cry for no reason, she was afraid of illnesses, she complained of pains all over her body, she was afraid of going out, of driving a car, of not being able to look after her children. She reported that she is often afraid when she goes to bed and turns off the light. At that moment, especially when her husband is away on business, she is afraid she might have some disease or other. She keeps on going over in her mind whether she closed the door, whether she set the alarm, whether the cars are in the garage, and where the children are. Then she remembers that they are sleeping in their room. At times of great loneliness, she takes her daughter or son into her bed for company.

Lia tells me that when she was very small, her mother used to travel a lot. Sometimes for two months at a time. During those periods, she would stay with nannies, aunts and uncles or grandparents.

She mentions cases of mental illness in the family that frightened her. They are painful memories that she does not like to recall. She describes her mother as very depressed. She mentions that currently there is a situation of conflict and distance from her mother and father, and she feels that she could not and cannot rely on them. Sunday nights are still terrible; she often falls into a void, a state of internal confusion, and the only thing that calms her down is the thought that she will see me on Monday.

She rarely misses a session and always tries to have interesting material to please me. She does not want me to worry because she is a heavy patient. She tries to forget the things that afflict her and escape her control, which she feels unable to cope with. By the time she comes to tell me about them they are emotionally distant, since she has already turned them into historical facts. It is quite common for her to begin the session by saying that she is sleepy, and often at the end of the session she is sad that something has been left out.

DR FERRO: Can we stop here for a bit, because we already have material enough for some reflections.

This material gives us a set of data which may be confirmed or not by the session. I was thinking about this hypochondriac aspect, the bodily pain, the fear of the dark, the uncertainty about whether she has shut the door or set the alarm. It is as if she were afraid that something terrible might suddenly burst into her reality, something whose vague presence she has already sensed, and therefore it is necessary to switch on an alarm that signals its arrival.

I wonder how we should think of this "thing" that is so feared. I am reminded of Bleger's notion of the agglutinated nucleus as something that precedes the paranoid-schizoid position, and it could be a good model to talk about this feared something that may burst into one's psychic life. In a different model, we might think of this "thing" as a cluster of items that I once called "betaloma"; a tumour-like formation of β elements whose sudden irruption into psychic life is feared, and makes necessary an alarm system that signals danger. This aggregate of β elements may correspond to the undigested facts that Bion talks about in *Learning from Experience*.[1]

The history of this patient sets us on this path: she had a mother who was often absent and depressed, so doubly unavailable, and could not introject a sufficient α function to metabolize β elements; both those that remained undigested historically, and those that are produced continuously day after day. I think that the fear of this depressed mother, a function that cannot be overloaded, also appears in the relationship with the analyst, where she tries to be a patient with interesting material that is not too much of a burden.

Thinking back to what we said yesterday, at times the presentation of the case already outlines a framework that can be

1 Bion, W. R. 1962. *Learning from Experience*. London: Heinemann.

thought of as the result of the analyst's waking dream thought; in a few lines, it gives us a kind of gist of his thoughts about the patient. It is as if, in his selection of the facts, the analyst were choosing those that already help us lay down a path.

ANALYST IN SUPERVISION: The session I am going to recount took place in October 1996. Lia has sessions from Monday to Thursday. This is a Wednesday. I also describe a short introductory section from the session immediately following this one.

*On Monday, Lia phoned me and said that something had come up and she couldn't come. For this session, the Wednesday one, she arrives on time, and then she lies down and talks to me slowly and at intervals.*

PATIENT: I'm depressed, with no desire to do anything, including the analysis. I have no will-power. Last night I had to breastfeed all the time; the baby woke up several times. I forgot to put the clock forward to summertime, and that's why I missed the appointment. This week the children have no lessons. I was too lazy to get up and I stood you up. I still think I have no friends. No one calls me. I can't stick to my diet. I remember that other times I had already managed to lose some weight by now.

*Later, Lia told me that she had been to two dinners, one on Friday and the other on Saturday, and that she had been out to lunch with friends and children on Sunday. She talks about a disagreement she had with her daughter at lunch that really annoyed her.*

ANALYST: You started talking about being downhearted.

*She interrupts me and says:*

PATIENT: I discussed Thursday with M. *(her husband)*, because that day we had a private viewing and M. told me he had a dinner. I didn't want him to go alone to the private viewing, nor did I want to go without him. He said: "So don't go".

So I went to a children's party. I met a girlfriend and we arranged to go together. I got home, I breastfed and went out. I stayed there for a while. I am always afraid of going out without M., of not being able to converse with people, but everything went well and my friend, who had said she didn't want to stay very long, wanted to leave and I left before M. arrived. I was glad I left alone. Half an hour later, M. came home and said: "For heaven's sake, I raced to meet you, but you had already gone". I said: "I stayed for a bit, but by then I was feeling all right and then I left". He was quite disappointed.

*She pauses and then goes on:*

PATIENT: Tonight, my daughter came to sleep in my bed and she slept with her head at the bottom of the bed: it took me some time to realize that it was her foot that was banging against my hand. I touched it and I woke up. My son woke up and he came into my room as well, saying he had not peed in the bed, although he had taken the feeding bottle.

ANALYST: It seems that you're talking about feeling dejected in various situations. You have not slept well, you have no friends, you cannot do your exercises or follow your diet, you missed your appointment, and you don't want to come here. At the same time, your son says that he is growing up, you make it to the private viewing and have several encounters with your friends.

PATIENT: When I don't come here and instead stay at home and sleep, I feel useless. It's hard to think that it's just because I'm tired. I missed the appointment because I was very tired. I remember that when I used to work I got home at six, and if I found my mother sleeping, I was upset.

*She pauses.*

PATIENT: I remembered a dream early this morning: I saw my very slim brother and I ran to ask him how he had managed to lose so much weight. He told me it was only by doing lots of exercise.

Yes, I can't stick to the diet, I always get demoralized and don't go to the gym; it's such an effort, I get downhearted. My brother didn't call me on T.'s birthday, or mine. I wanted to talk to him and find out what is happening, because he is so fat. I am very upset. I don't think people should be fat.

ANALYST: It seems to me that in this dream there is a desire for change, but in a magical way, without much effort. But you yourself realize that you need to do plenty of exercise, to make a big effort to deal with all the emotions that are inside you. It takes lots of practice.

*She agrees and takes a break.*

PATIENT: I'm thinking that I'm tired now, but I'm not really sleepy. All the time I've been singing that song by Simone, "Risuscitami" ("Revive me"). I can't get it out of my head.

*The words of the song are as follows:*

> Maybe, who knows, one day from an avenue at the zoo, she too will come,
> She too, who loved animals, will come in smiling as in the photo on the table.
> She is so beautiful that they will certainly revive her.
> In the thirtieth century the heart now broken by meanness will win.
> So now, we will achieve everything we cannot wish for in life.
> With the starry sky of countless nights,
> Revive me although I am no longer,
> because I am a poet and I yearned for the future.
> Revive me struggling against the miseries of daily life.
> Revive me then,
> Revive me. I want to finish living what is mine,
> My life, because there are no slavish loves.
> Revive me, because no one should sacrifice themselves for a house,
> For a hole.
> Revive me, because starting from today, starting from today the family
> transforms,
> And the father is at least the universe and the mother is at least the Earth, the Earth.

PATIENT: "Risuscitami". I can't get it out of my head.

ANALYST: It's interesting, because from the beginning I thought there was a tone to what you said, a feeling of despair, and the idea of this song is that together we can recover hope.

PATIENT: I am reminded of something Garfield said about diets: "You can't spell diet without 'die'." *(Laughs)* He is always making interesting remarks about diets, especially when he is eating lasagne.

ANALYST: It seems that something has happened between us. You've found a lively tone and a good mood inside yourself.

*Here are the opening moments of the next session.*

PATIENT: I have backache. I think that the sadness of yesterday also has to do with being married for ten years. It's my wedding anniversary today. I think it's really nice when you see a father and a mother celebrating ten, twenty years of marriage. All I'm afraid of is that something nasty will happen. There are people who don't even manage to stay married for a year. We have built our marriage on a different basis from my parents. We have three children; that's a lot. I think this has affected me in some way. Nice, I thought when I celebrated it, but the feeling is not as strong as when it's my birthday, or M.'s birthday, or the children's. Every day I celebrate my marriage, I fight for it. Yesterday, we were out for dinner and we discussed it, and I said to M. that our marriage is good because we fight every day. When it was past midnight, we tried to remember what we had done the night before our wedding, and he was the one who remembered that we went out for a pizza.

ANALYST: Did you feel close to him?

PATIENT: Time affects me: ten years; the time that passes; the knowledge that I'm thirty-five and not twenty-five or thirty. I think if it was good, it was worth it, if I did everything I wanted. Not everything is perfect. This is a bit too much, but there are lots of things wrong, things I have to adjust, how to go to a private viewing on my own, the thing that costs me most effort, and without M. it is difficult. There are things to fix. I remembered that on Monday. M. had some trouble at work, and his boss was away on business. I told him: "You'll find a solution". He said that in this case there was no solution, but I told him that I was sure he could do it. He was very downhearted, then he came back really happy because he had found a solution.

ANALYST: Speaking of M, you seem to feel confident that he will overcome difficulties, and you're starting to find within yourself the belief and the hope that you will be able to feel alive and be transformed.

DR FERRO: Before looking at the sequence, I would like to suggest some theoretical reflections on the session. I have some difficulty speaking about it, because I agree with what my colleague said. I don't know if it is a habitual style, or whether it is especially true in this session, but the analyst does not sing in parallel with the patient's speaking. She doesn't say: "you said this", "you said that" etc. In the session there is no attitude of decoding what the patient says, and the analyst is not worried about finding, or especially explaining, the hidden meaning of the patient's communication. This process often creates a variation of the field, meaning that we are told what the patient wants to say, coupled with the manner in which she listened to the analyst's interventions; that is, to the dream the patient makes out of what the analyst says.

A way of working that stays close to what the patient says, and takes into full account their manifest verbal communication, allows the patient to gradually boost their capacity for thought, enabling the analysis to be the probe that can expand the field it is exploring, as Bion puts it, and puts the patient at the forefront of this exploration.

What I mean by this is not that the analyst should not interpret, but that he must have great respect for the patient's manifest communication, and also the patience to wait for the patient to explore, little by little, their ability to think. So, as we said this morning,[2] my idea is that an analyst should stay in Row C of the Grid, moving in the direction of C3, C4, C5, focusing the patient's attention on something that they have said; above all shedding light, inviting the patient to reflect on something that they have already communicated, refusing to explain every possible relational meaning. However, it is important that the analyst be aware in their own mind of these relational meanings. I continue to think that the analyst within themself should guide the material in the direction of D, E and F on the Grid — but there should be no need to communicate it to the patient immediately.

With regard to the dream in which the patient sees her brother who has been on a diet and sees how he has managed to lose weight, a possible interpretation could have been that missing the Monday session corresponded to the lack of food that made the brother lose weight. But I don't feel the need to communicate this to the patient, nor to talk about having to console the child who was crying all night long, or wanting to be breastfed. I think it is essential, however, that the analyst has all these meanings in mind

2 See Clinical Seminar IV.

and knows that, behind the private viewing, there is a girl who always dreams of being breastfed; there is weight loss owing to missing the session. I believe that the analyst has thought about all this because the first interpretation focuses on the patient's sense of despondency. After this first intervention, the patient seems to feel more relieved.

Following the images that appear in the session — not as images that have a direct link to what the patient has done or stopped doing in external reality, but as something that reflects the atmosphere of the relationship at the moment when these images are narrated — comes the children's party, a friend she has arranged to go out with … At this point, we could interpret either by saying "You see me as the friend you can count on", or "My words came across to you as a moment of encounter", but that would be the parallel song I mentioned earlier.

The patient's communications can be seen as a dream image of the current relational situation. However, this relational signal does not have to be interpreted; all there should be is an attempt to receive the emotional quality of the patient's response as something that can guide the way we carry on talking with them.

By refraining from decoding interpretations in his subsequent intervention, the analyst is able to continue working in Row C, in the direction of C4, C5. I say Row C, because I think that the analyst does not look at the reality of these communications, but thinks of them as emotional communications in the relational field, and makes an intervention that comes closer to the different emotional states of the patient. At this point, what begins to emerge is what could not be thought; it seems to me, namely, that this is a patient who never wants to go underground, never wants to go to a lower level — minus one, minus two, minus three — and the analyst may be tempted, from the beginning of the session, to go straight to level minus ten. Then, the patient would only feel highly persecuted and would head straight for level fifteen.

I think there should be a great deal of respect for the patient's defences and for Column 2 of the Grid; it is sufficient that it is the patient telling the lie and that the lie is a defence against something that terrifies them. If the analyst has this negative capability to tolerate more superficial levels, to accept that the analysis can go to a private viewing, and if it makes the patient feel that there is someone with them in the lift, the patient may find the courage to begin to drop down, feeling this as their own personal choice and not as something imposed.

In fact, this is the point in the session where the dream appears in which the patient sees her brother, who has lost a lot of weight, and goes up to him to ask him how he did it. In other words, separation anxiety, fear of abandonment, fear of having a child with a very depressed mother, with a mentally absent parent, who is therefore not good nourishment for the mind of the child — all this appears, through the dream, as something the patient can think of, whereas if the analyst had machine-gunned her at the beginning of the session with an interpretation about separation anxiety or missing the session, this would have produced only denial, or a sense of persecution in the patient.

I am increasingly convinced that being in O with the patient is not so much a matter of content or truth, but rather a matter of being in unison with the patient, being on the same emotional wavelength. It's as if, every time, the truth only comes from one mind, even when it is a "true" and thought truth, for the patient it is always -K. In this case, however, we see a patient who, little by little, can achieve a truth she can share with the analyst.

I find it poetic when she says "Revive me" *(risuscitami)*. Let us not forget that there has been a history of a depressed and absent mother. For this patient, separation is something terrible; she feels alone, abandoned. But then, at some point, she manages to have a less catastrophic, even ironic and creative view of things; she is able to distinguish between diet and death: "Diet is 'die' with a t" — and to discriminate creatively between missing a session (going on a diet) and death, reflecting on the fact that missing a session is not death, that being alone, the times when her husband is away on a trip, is not the end of everything. It is as if here there were a transformation of a catastrophic anxiety, to which you just need to add a "t" to make it something that is certainly not exactly cheerful — like, for example, a diet — but something one can put up with. There is also the way she testifies to feeling the close, accompanying presence of this analyst, reflected in the emotional exchange about eating lasagne.

What I also find interesting is her concern at the beginning of the next session that now that there has been a good encounter, something terrible might happen. It is as if what previously was anxiety about catastrophic death — and which then became a diet or a loss — were then transformed into a reflection by the patient about the nature of time. At this moment, I am reminded of a wonderful observation by Winnicott, who I think you'll know, and that goes something like: "Only now do I realize how many achievements I have prevented my patients from making, owing to my great need to interpret; now I realize that I am thrilled more by the amount of truth patients are able to discover by themselves than by the pleasure of telling them the truth."

The analyst's function may be to act as an enzyme that catalyzes transformations in the consulting room. This does not exclude the fact that there are situations that require direct interpretations, transference interpretations, highly saturated interpretations or content interpretations. But these two sessions have shown how a patient is able to transform death anxiety into loss anxiety, or anxiety about the passage of time, and how the analyst's interventions can promote this development without having to decode meaning.

The utility of a historical reconstruction of the patient's childhood experience with the mother remains an open question, as does the question of whether it is necessary to explicate these very deep death anxieties. But I think, at this moment, it is more important to encourage these transformations rather than putting the patient into a "descending lift", and plunging sharply to level minus twelve. I am very confident that patients, as they gradually gain courage and see that nothing serious happens as they go down gradually, will end up descending on their own, or asking to be accompanied to the lower levels of their psychic life.

I would now like to hear your impressions of the session and what has been said so far.

AUDIENCE: How old is the child?

ANALYST IN SUPERVISION: Five months.

AUDIENCE: I was interested by your way of looking at the analyst's task in this session. As I understand it, you positioned it in Row C of the Grid, and in movement with regard to attention, investigation, notation … I am pleased to hear you speak so clearly on what has become a taboo issue in psychoanalysis; namely, the place of interpretation today. That is to say, interpretation occupies a relatively narrow space in the work of the analyst, and the important task has become not to saturate the field and to set up conditions conducive to transformations in the patient, where the field is wide so as to allow transformations to occur.

I have been asking myself what the analyst does today. When he's not interpreting, what does he do? I was satisfied with your proposal, although this analyst is perhaps not always very conscious of what he is doing. However, I believe that many analyses — and the session in question is quite interesting from this point of view — are much more like this conversation. A conversation which is apparently almost symmetrical, with no great revelations, nothing very "bruising". In other words, a perfectly ordinary situation. Most of the time analysis limits itself to this, perhaps with the occasional moment that may be interpretive.

AUDIENCE: I would like to emphasize two points that took my attention. The first is that there is a vantage point of the analyst which in some way allows her to see what is called a "werecat", and, in some way, the analyst realizes that her role is not to be a detective or a hunter of those not present at the session. The second point is something that is not clear, but that I would want to investigate with the patient: it is the moment when she is lying in bed, just as she lies in the room, and is confused as to whether she is holding the child's head or feet. This moment, which has something to do with some kind of contact, points to something confusing or disruptive: possible problems of identity; possibly the problems of how a wife who has maternal functions may also have other functions.

AUDIENCE: In this session my attention was drawn to the frequent allusions to breastfeeding, and this patient's need to be fed by the analyst, by her friend, by her husband. I would like to know how to deal with this, since this is a patient with predominantly depressive symptoms. I'm thinking of the historical or genetic part of the patient.

AUDIENCE: Hearing Dr Ferro talk, I think we can both interpret and perform other types of intervention, but it seems that, whichever attitude we take, there is a price to pay. If we interpret the patient's missing the session, this would have a similar effect to what he pointed out. If we didn't interpret it, the sequence would be different. Could it be that the price is announced at the beginning of the other session; for example, as backache?

DR FERRO: There are many open questions, but first let me clarify a few things about Row C. We can be in Row C of the Grid with the patient as long as we listen to the patient's communications, not as communications about the facts of their external life, or of what happens in their inner world, but as an ongoing account of what is happening in the consulting room. In this way, by not saturating the field, I believe that the truth will appear as a discursive truth, without there being any moments of interpretive caesura; for example, the problem of the child lying upside down in bed.

Of course, we can think of this as something that, in fact, happened at night in bed with the patient's son, and then of her maternal qualities etc. But the point of view I prefer is that the patient is saying that there is an adult lying on the couch in the right direction, and an infantile part that has its head at the wrong end, without my knowing why, or what it means. Certainly, the aspect I privilege — and which is why I feel I am in Row C — is that this communication is a double functioning of the patient inside the consulting room. We still do not know what meaning to give her, but this little girl lying upside down is something to keep in mind.

The same applies to breastfeeding and feeding, both when the patient talks about breastfeeding the baby and when she talks about the analyst, the girlfriend, the husband etc. If I want to stay in the C row, I have to think about these relationships, not as facts concerning the patient's external life, but in terms of all modes of operation inside the consulting room, as if there were different relational vectors in the field.

Of course, there is a problem of depression in the patient, and this is what I meant when I talked about the lift going down, and there is still a very complacent level in her that, for the moment, prevents her from descending towards all the strong negative feelings — anger, aggression, everything that is linked to abandonment — that she is not yet able to talk about. A child cannot be born if the head is not in the correct position: it first needs to be manoeuvred into place. Undoubtedly, there are levels of great anger, great suffering, great frustration that must come out.

I am convinced that what my colleague said earlier is true; namely, that each approach has its price. If we think of the analytic situation in field terms, however the analyst behaves in the session, they will produce, along with the patient, the transformations that occur in the field. The important thing is to be aware of this, to pick up the signals that the field constantly sends out, and to try to intervene in the most constructive and least costly way possible. Undoubtedly, however, there is a cost. For the analyst, there is no neutral way of being; whatever their position, they will, together with the patient, produce transformations in the field.

AUDIENCE: In some of your previous observations you made the point that when the analyst is there for the patient and is more or less in tune with them, in ordinary conversation about concrete facts, there begins a phase where the object is more integrated. In the process of association, we can try to grasp the deeper aspects, undigested β elements. By way of an exercise, let me pose the following question: when the patient speaks of the son she touched, in my mind I had a sort of free association; I thought of a pelvic birth, of asphyxia, something related to some internal confusion. Could this be regarded as a β element that can now be digested, as a way of searching for the meaning of this confusion?

AUDIENCE: Could you say something about "weak interpretation?".

DR FERRO: Let me start from this question about weak interpretation. I had to go on a long journey to get to this way of thinking about the importance of sharing a narrative with the patient. I came from a training that put the emphasis on content interpretations. Then I went though a series of key moments that made me change. I remember a very serious child who suffered from hallucinations. Once, during the session, he drew an armchair with two buttons on the back. I remember saying that they were two breasts with nipples. At that time, he was hallucinating and, in his first insight, he looked at me stunned and said, "Are you crazy? This is a chair".

I must confess that this trivial episode has continued to resonate within me. After some time, I realized that we were both right, but there is a big difference between saying to the patient "This is a breast with a nipple" and saying "Ah, finally, we can draw a comfortable armchair in this room". It is clear that, in my mind, the comfortable armchair has to do with hospitality, with availability, with the place … It has to do with the fact of being looked at and being seen, but this refers to the analyst's internal map. For the patient, it is more useful to say: "Ah, at last a comfortable armchair".

Years later, another patient came along, who was always telling me about the difficulties she had relating to her boyfriend, and I interpreted everything she said about him in a rigid way, in terms of the transference. Everything she told me about her boyfriend I transposed onto me. One day, this patient asked if she could have a word before lying down on the couch: "Look, there's something I've been meaning to say for a long time. When I enter this room, I enter with one problem, namely, my boyfriend. When I leave the room, I go out with two problems: the problem with my boyfriend, plus the one I have with you. What's in it for me?". This is another episode that has stayed in my mind. I then understood that it was necessary to speak to patients in such a way that they really feel helped, and that the most important thing is the quality of the transformation. This realization formed the basis for what a colleague and I began to call narrative or weak interpretations,[3] which do not saturate the patient's communication but are a bit like Lego. The idea was to offer the patient one of those small building blocks with their multiple possible uses, in such a way as to avoid saturating the field.

However, as our colleague said earlier, it is sometimes possible to go too far in this direction and I remember an incident with a patient of the colleague who was working with me on weak interpretations: he had a dream where someone was tied to a post ready to be shot. The situation was terrible, because the people with the rifle were always there but they never fired.

There is no situation where only unsaturated interpretations are appropriate. There is a constant oscillation between the negative capability of the analyst, their being able to remain in the PS position without feeling persecuted, and the need for a selected fact, provided that the selected fact really arises from an emotion that the analyst feels there and then. I thought about what Bion says about interpretation; that it must cover the field of sense, myth and passion. This means that it is necessary to interpret something the patient can touch and see, something that must be there. If there is no "sensual" factor, there is no point in interpreting. I would add: not only is there PS↔PD oscillation,

3 Bezoari, M. & Ferro, A. 1999. "Ascolto, interpretazioni e funzioni trasformative nel dialogo analitico". *Rivista Psicoanalitica*, XXXV, 4, 1015–1051.

but there is also the continuous oscillation between the analyst's negative capability and the need for a selected fact.

In relation to the question I was asked a while ago, I mentioned this morning[4] what Bion says about the ability to develop the container: the container is formed when a network of emotions develops. For me, this is the network that is formed between analyst and patient, and this is what is created when there is emotional attunement between analyst and patient. But when you develop a container, unavoidably, at some point, content also develops, which means that even the most primitive anxieties can be transformed. We should not go hunting for content, but we should create the prerequisites that allow content to take shape in the session, ensuring that ever deeper and more changeable anxieties and β elements may appear gradually.

4 See Clinical Seminar IV.

# Clinical Seminar VI

ANALYST IN SUPERVISION: D. is a girl of eleven years of age. Her father is an engineer and an entrepreneur. Her mother is a teacher but does not work. When they came to see me in August 1995, D. was attending the fifth year of a very strict school. Then, in 1996, she was sent to a school that was more appropriate to her level of development.

The parents came to see me on returning from a trip to Europe. They were very anxious because while they were away there had been evidence of the child's disorders: D.'s marks at school had gone down a lot, she cried every night and insisted that her grandmother take her to the best restaurants in town. The parents phoned every night and she blackmailed them by asking for gifts. I had a countertransference experience that the child was trying to stifle her great anguish with "things".

The family, native to southern Brazil, has suffered numerous bereavements and has often had to move. When the patient was still very young, her mother's brother died, followed by her godfather. The way the family found to cope with these painful situations was to give her a doll her godfather had bought. She took the doll for the real godfather. It wasn't just a pretend version; for her, it really was the godfather.

Her mother's pregnancy with her only brother was very dramatic, because she had suffered a detachment of the placenta with the result that she was bedridden for many months. During that period, her father would leave her at the home of her maternal grandmother, and go to pick her up in the evening. When she came back home, she would cry and ask her mother to hold her, but her mother was unable to do anything too strenuous.

The mother is frustrated because she has stopped practising her profession in order to be a wife, hostess and good mother, but she is deemed to have failed to cope with the innumerable problems presented by D., who threatens to kill herself every time some constraint or rule is imposed on her.

In the first hour of play, D. seemed to me to be an extremely childish girl with severe phobic features, who was experiencing emptiness and unworked-through grief. She called my attention to the way she coped with this emptiness: beneath the paranoid-schizoid position, I could sense a deep depression.

We started with three sessions a week and have continued at the same rhythm ever since.

I chose the session I'm going to describe because in it I had to deal with a special situation, which comes out in the question of the setting, involving two factors: on the one hand, what might be psychopathic manipulation, to circumvent situations of distress and anxiety; and on the other, the problem of helping the child to live and cope with limitations and frustrations, and to face up to these anxieties and this feeling of emptiness in other ways.

To explain the background for this session, I should mention a difficulty I experienced on the level of transference on an occasion six months before the session I am going to recount. The mother called me shortly before the session to tell me that D. was very ill, could not come and that she was going to take her to the doctor's, which is what indeed happened. The mother asked to reschedule the session, and while talking with her, I realized she was very anxious. I had an hour free the next day and said she could come then. I was able to see D.'s attitude clearly, and the mother was able to observe her with me. That day her parents were due to go to a wedding in another city, 100 kilometres away, but they cancelled because of D.'s condition, although it turned out to be something so minor that the doctor did not even ask for tests. Moreover, when she came to me, the girl did not even have a temperature.

When D. arrived at the session, she said: "I thought that coming to the session was like having a cup of tea when I don't feel well. But what happened was not at all bad, because my parents didn't go to the wedding. And if I had come here, I knew that I would have to think". I worked on the problem of trying to discover simultaneously the meaning and the use she made of her pain. I suggested that perhaps it was good to have that session to talk about all this, but that perhaps it was also important that she should learn to lose, and to see what she was doing with all her manipulations.

At the present moment, we are facing a new situation: her parents are due to go to a conference connected to her father's job and, as a reward, they have invited her to go with them. Here in Brazil, on October 12, we celebrate *Nossa Senhora Aparecida* and Children's Day. This year, the holiday fell on a Saturday. She never has sessions on Saturdays but decided she wanted to transform the 14th (Monday) into a holiday, as some schools do in celebration of Children's Day, and to have a week's vacation mid-year. Since she will be travelling and will not have class, she wants me to turn this day into a holiday, or if I go to work, to give her an appointment on another day, so as not to miss the session. However, the first thing she says is: "Why aren't you on holiday on the 14th?". I explained that Monday for me was a normal working day and that I would be working: school is school, analysis is analysis. I showed her that she was mixing things up, and that the trip was a reward granted by her family, but she would not get the session back.

She has sessions on Mondays, Tuesdays and Wednesdays. The session I am going to describe was on Wednesday, two weeks before the trip.

*Upon arriving, she draws a boat, the moon and a small person at the bottom asking for help.*

*Figure 6*

*She talks of the hotel where the family will stay on this trip, which means not working on Monday the 14th. She also tells me that her father has managed to book a connecting room. The hotel does not accept more than two people in one room, but another girl would sleep with her so that she wouldn't be alone. This was how I learned that her father wanted her next door (in the adjacent room) to avoid tears or anguish.*

ANALYST: You may feel like this girl here, who is drowning, and who appears to feel very weak and threatened, threatened by a session.

*She says she told her mother that she would have preferred to be the younger child. Her mother replied that if she had been, she would have got very angry because of all the things the older child was capable of doing. So then she told her mother that she would rather have been the middle child. And her mother told her that then she wouldn't have been given any attention and that her brothers would have been the ones to be looked after.*

ANALYST: Do you feel that you don't have a quiet place where you can understand that you are really loved? I think this is the question.

*She says she quarrelled with her brother, who pushed her after she had provoked him. The mother said that by way of punishment she would not be able to sleep over at her friend's house. This is the second time she has been punished in this way and cannot take up her friend's invitation. Last time, she had to celebrate her birthday with her grandparents, who were visiting the city.*

ANALYST: You do not feel recognized as someone capable of being a proper eleven year old, being away from her parents, putting up with one fewer session …

PATIENT: My mother said if I had not wanted to change schools, she would have respected my wishes. My brother did not want to change. But, because of me, my mother moved him too.

*(This has to do with the beginning of the process: D. was doing badly at a very demanding school that was too difficult for her. The parents had to go through a long process to make D. accept being put into a school more suited to her emotional development at that time. And the mother, to save time and to makes things easier, decided to change the son's school as well.)*

PATIENT: I would prefer to be alone. Now I do not need to sleep with so many blankets, it's as if I could accept it. Okay, it's nice, so

I'm not even arguing with my father. I say that he is calmer now. My mother says I am calmer. Well, it's not a question of chicken and the egg.

ANALYST: Now that you are more confident and sure of yourself, you don't need so many blankets in order to feel secure and whole.

*She does the part of the drawing "My Brother", then writes EU, and at one end of the letter U she puts a bottle on one side and a cup on the other. At the other end, she draws the rocket and the explosion. She says that her brother called their mother Pinocchio because of her nose, and because the mother doesn't like it.*

ANALYST: But it's like you exploded in anger because you stayed out of this relationship between your mother and your brother. What is our truth? Who will I be with on the 14th? Do I want your presence or am I leaving you out, apart?

*She begins to turn the moon into a scribble.*

PATIENT: I wanted Snoopy to come to my house and my brother to stay in the country house.

ANALYST: Forget about your brother and the other patients … and that way you'll guarantee yourself a place in my heart. *(At this point, I realize how different she is, more grown-up: the child has become a girl with earrings, bracelets, a pendant and a T-shirt with a heart.)*

*She writes "UAU" on the waves of the sea. She also says that she likes her brother, that on Saturday her parents are going to a wedding and her brother has a birthday party at the Hípica (a club). She doesn't want him to go to the party and wants him to keep her company. If the brother doesn't stay at home, she will stay with a friend. She doesn't want to be home alone.*

ANALYST: Perhaps you scare yourself when you realize that you want to push out this brother, but you also understand that you need him, just like you need the work here, to help you keep your own company.

*(This question of having company also has a history. I asked her to describe how she felt when she was alone, and she described it as something terrible: she needed to turn on the lights and to cover herself with four blankets because she was afraid that thieves and ghosts might come, and that she might not find anything to grab hold of. At night, all the soft toys in her room, which she liked so much during the day, turned into ghosts. At that moment, I had shown her that she had nothing inside her to keep her company.)*

PATIENT *(laughing a lot)*: Keep going.

ANALYST: I think the desperation of this exploding sun is you in the air or drowned in anguish, while you imagine your brother glued to your mother, or to me, in ecstasy! That's what makes you explode and then you start elbowing, kicking, pushing, like someone saying: "I want my own little corner in this world".

DR FERRO: I don't want to do a supervision of the session in the strict sense of the word. I have the impression that the session contains great movement and great transformation, and one can progressively see how this child feels helped by the analysis. I don't want to interfere in the work the analyst is doing in such a creative way with the patient, using a very consistent model.

What I would like to do, however, is to use this material as the basis for an exercise; that is, I want to change the model, to look at the material in another way. By that, however, I don't want to say that this way is better than that of the analyst. It's just another way to see this material, or at least, it's my way of feeling this material.

I think this child suffered major harm very early. She suffered a lot from the emotional distance of her parents, especially the period of the mother's unavailability while she was pregnant with her brother; a period when the mother felt worried about her brother, and was mentally preoccupied with the pregnancy. I think that on top of this wound there formed a kind of perversion, character disorder, narcissism; a behaviour pattern that could also be thought of as having the characteristics of anal masturbation. But I would like to emphasize another point of view. A very deep wound can scar over or can form a keloid, excessive scarring. There are two points of view, that of the analyst and that of the patient, and the latter has used this keloid to cover over this wound temporarily, as if the child were constantly forced to heal her wounds.

Let us consider two factors that emerge from the drawing. The first is the way of understanding the characters of the session, and the second is the attention paid to how to consider the reaction of the child to the analyst's interpretations. On the first point, there are various ways in which the characters can be understood: as external, as real, as belonging to the inner world, or as characters who constantly tell us what is going on inside the session. Perhaps you remember *Finnegans Wake* by James Joyce, which has a constantly changing narrative mode: nothing is definitive, the characters are in a state of continuous transformation.

I agree that in this drawing we have the question of the child drowning, but I wonder if there might not be a less saturated way of formulating the problem: by not putting it at the forefront, but leaving it for the moment at the margins, belonging to Row C of the Grid, but without focusing on C4 or C5.

In the story of the hotel that only accepts two people per room — the story of the joint room — we have a girl that asks how this hotel/consulting room works, because for her the analysis is a hotel where always being united is compulsory. I would have pointed out this aspect to the girl, who asks whether it is possible to change the rules of the hotel, whether it is possible to miss a session without this amounting to a tragedy. In which respect, she is the opposite to her father, who is anxious to have her sleep in the adjoining room so as to avoid tears and anguish. I would see the father, in this *Finnegans Wake* type of reading, as one of the ways in which the analyst could be represented.

I have the impression that the analyst feels it is his duty to catch the drowning child. Certainly it is something that exists in the field. But we see how the patient responds when the analyst focuses attention on this point and makes an interpretation. The patient's response comes directly from their waking dream thought; that is to say, the analyst interprets and the patient immediately forms a series of α elements connected to this interpretation. The patient cannot know her α elements, but somehow brings out the narrative derivatives of her α elements. The narrative derivative that comes out here is this: I would like to be the younger child, and the mother says that the younger child is full of anger because the older child is capable of doing. Looked at from this point of view, it is as if the patient said that after this interpretation she feels like the younger child, who is very angry at everything the elder brother-analyst is in a position to tell her.

Then, when the analyst says: "You feel that you have no quiet place where you feel really loved", we can look at the response of the patient as a narrative derivative of the waking dream thought. I do not know whether this idea is clear …

Analyst in supervision: The idea is not very clear. Could you explain it in more depth?

DR FERRO: The analyst interprets, the patient forms α elements, the α element is unknowable, and the narrative derivative of the α element appears.

AUDIENCE: Are α elements being produced all the time?

DR FERRO: According to Bion's theory, all of us, including the people here, constantly produce α elements, and each of these α elements is a vignette that sums up, in an original and creative way, the emotional experience of the relationship we are experiencing at this moment.

AUDIENCE: But if the patient is in a paranoid-schizoid phase, she will not be able to hear the analyst's interpretation. Won't she then be producing only β elements and not α elements?

DR FERRO: Can I reply to that later? I would like to finish explaining my first idea.

According to Bion in *Learning from Experience*,[1] waking dream thought is a process that goes on continuously. We form one α element after another in sequence. The α element sums up the whole of our experience at that moment. If we think that, at this moment, something good is happening, the α element will be a piping hot pizza. If, however, we are bored by what is going on, the α element will be different. Every day the Italian newspaper, *La Repubblica*, publishes a cartoon on the front page that is based on that day's most important events.

Waking dream thought is always at work, except in those serious situations when the patient is neither awake nor asleep: situations of confused oneiric delusion. Otherwise, according to Bion, there is always a waking dream thought in operation that forms the "contact barrier" that allows us to distinguish our unconscious from the perception of external reality.

To go on to the question of the narrative derivative: for example, I make an interpretation to a patient, saying that it seems to me that behind their anger lies great despair. This patient has a dream-like flash and looking at a picture of a landscape on the wall opposite, they say: "My God, I see a mask being taken off". At that moment, the patient's α element, triggered by my interpretation, is a mask being taken off.

However, it is exceptional for the element to jump out and be seen like this. It happens in those patients who have visual flashes

1 Bion, W. R. 1962. *Learning from Experience*. London: Heinemann.

that are not hallucinations. Generally, patients have no visual flashes, in which case the element is inside. With a patient whose α element remains inside, instead of this visual image we only have its narrative derivative; for example, "When I was a child, a friend tore off my favourite dress". This is the difference between the α element and the narrative derivative of the α element.

So, I propose that we regard the patient's response as full of α elements whose narrative derivative it is possible to know.

AUDIENCE: I have a question about the theoretical-conceptual plane. In your book *The Bi-personal Field. Experiences in Child Psychoanalysis*,[2] you talk about the mystic writing pad as a model of Freud's that has been made obsolete by Bion. In his paper on the mystic writing pad, Freud adds an element that is not part of the mystic writing pad:[3] the unconscious has a kind of antenna that always picks up the objective, concrete data that are on the same wavelength. What, then, is the difference between Freud's view and the α elements?

DR FERRO: Can I answer that question later? First, I would like to conclude my reflections on the session.

Following the analyst's interpretation ("You feel you have no safe place"), the child says she quarrelled with her brother, who had pushed her because he had provoked her first. If we look at the level of the matrix that generates language and emotion, we can imagine this answer as the narration of the fact that the patient feels touched and distanced from her brother; her brother-analyst. All of this has happened within the relationship.

The session continues: "You do not feel recognized", says the analyst, "because you cannot bear having one less session". At this point, another dream thought appears in response, because she speaks of the change in school as if the narrative derivative of the patient's dream thought, after interpretation, had registered the fact that the analyst had changed his way of relating to her and she had switched to a less demanding school. We have two schools: on the one hand, the school as bottle and cup; on the other, the school as rocket and explosion. I would also see the bottle and the cup,

2 Ferro, A. 1999. *The Bi-personal Field. Experiences in Child Psychoanalysis*. London: Routledge.

3 Freud S. "A Note upon the 'Mystic Writing-Pad'." (1925). In: Strachey, J. (Ed.). 1961. *The Standard Edition of Freud's Works,* Vol. 19, London: Hogarth Press. pp. 227–232.

the rocket and the explosion, as narrative derivatives of the dream thought. More classically, we could say that the patient responds: "You, the analyst, you act with me in two ways: one is nutritional and containing (the bottle and cup); and in the other I'm hit and I feel myself exploding".

When the analyst interprets: "... if you exploded with anger etc...." she scribbles the sun. The patient comes back to these two schools (the cup and bottle school, and the rocket and explosion school) under the names "Snoopy and brother". I see *Snoopy* as a transformation of the bottle and the cup, a way in which the patient feels in unison, and *brother* as something that has more to do with the rocket.

I like the analyst's interpretation when he says: "You want to eliminate your brother in order to ensure you have a place in your mother's heart". But I would see the brother as this "rocket" function of the session; a way of finding a place more easily in the analyst's heart.

At this point, if we continue this approach, after the interpretation in which the patient seems to feel the analyst close and available, we see the narrative derivative of the girl's dream thought. The brother ceases to be persecutory but is someone she likes, there is a wedding, her brother goes to a party and she would like her brother to keep her company, and again she experiences the analyst as a friend she would like to be with. Things change constantly, relational moment by relational moment, as if there were a photographer who, at any given moment, took photographs from totally unpredictable angles.

I like the interpretation where the analyst says, "You are scared when you realize you want to eliminate your brother, but also when you understand that you need him". It is a classic transference interpretation. The analyst picks up these two aspects, Snoopy and the brother, bottle and rocket, which could also be the two ways in which the child sees the analyst: someone she is afraid of; and someone she needs. When the child feels the analyst close to her, she asks him to speak more, to use a little more bottle and cup.

I would like to hear your opinions.

AUDIENCE: If the patient is in a persecutory situation, she is deprived momentarily of the possibility of having the $\alpha$ function: she is producing $\beta$ elements and is not even able to feel what the analyst says. I would like you to talk about my hypothesis that often there is no α function, either for the patient or for the analyst. How, then, can we see these visual or narrative elements? Do they not perhaps always correspond to Row C, and are thus processed by the α function?

Now, a little joke. It seems that Brazilian patients are always hallucinating, they have transformations in hallucinosis, and they have almost no waking dream thoughts.

AUDIENCE: Not for all analysts …

DR FERRO: Why must we think that the α function operates only in D (the Depressive position) and that in PS the patient does not produce any α elements? I don't think this is the case, and I don't think that Bion says it anywhere. Moreover, Bion has high regard for PS, both when he says that mental health is not a movement from PS in the direction of D but is rather a constant oscillation, and when he speaks of negative capability as the ability of the analyst to continue in PS without feeling a sense of persecution.

I believe that the α function of the patient, their waking dream thought and that of the analyst (even in low doses) is almost always present, except in situations where the patient's mind disintegrates and they have real hallucinations. Then there is an inversion of the α function, and pieces of mind are evacuated along with pieces of α elements, generating bizarre objects. But that is what happens in cases of serious pathology.

On the other question … really, I don't know how to answer. I am very fond of *Learning from Experience*. I think it is Bion's most extraordinary book, even more extraordinary than all the others that followed. *Learning from Experience* is full of deeply innovative thinking. Chapters VII and VIII describe in minute detail the operation of waking dream thought, the formation of the α element, the contact barrier, as something that serves to distinguish what is conscious from what is unconscious.

I think the fundamental difference between Freud and Bion is that, for Bion, the unconscious is formed by the α function working on the β element. The β element is unknowable, and the α element operates on it. Some α elements are like a drawing you can see, and they form what is sufficiently conscious. The unconscious is downstream from the relationship with the other.

AUDIENCE: In this different view of the material, another aspect to discuss would be what role the α elements have for this child. In this sense, the drowning girl would be a way in which she feels she must convey these α elements to someone who can do something (in this case, the analyst), who would then move towards abandoning a mental function on the part of the child. In short, there is a whole way of viewing the session from this perspective. For example, when the mother sends her to an easier school, does this not mean that the child is saying she needs the analyst to say something more concrete? In this sense, Freud's notion of the unconscious does not seem to me to be something already formed, because the child too, as in Joyce's book, takes shape in a relationship.

Dr Ferro: For example, in order to see how this kind of anguish could be transformed I could ask the girl who is drowning, "What's happening?". At times, the analyst sees many true things, but … the same thing can happen as with a piece of film, which burns if it is exposed to more light than it can withstand.

It would be necessary to activate an α function, which for the moment I shall call the α function of the field, which belongs neither to the patient nor to the analyst, and which makes possible continuous transformations of the huge quantity of the patient's β elements and undigested facts, through a synergistic process of the patient's and the analyst's α function. But they really have to work in synergy with each other.

I agree with the idea that the reference to changing school could well be a desire on the part of the patient to change the analyst's words into something more concrete. I know I am looking at things from a very special angle of vision and, moreover, in the session there is a series of positive changes that I do not want to disturb. In addition to *Finnegans Wake*, there are other types of functioning, like *Ulysses*, or the *Divine Comedy*, all with different narrative possibilities. This is one way of looking at the material, but it is not the only one; there are many more.

Audience: You know that our group has been meeting to read your book, *Experiences in Child Analysis*,[4] and there has been much debate, even heated debate.

Dr Ferro: Thank you.

4 Ferro, A. 1999. *The Bi-Personal Field: Experiences in Child Analysis*. London, New York: Routledge.

AUDIENCE: Part of our discussion centred on the fact that you always gave only a short excerpt from the session, and that you favoured the patient's reply over interpretation. The only thing is that we have never been given a full session, such as we have here, where you are working on all the material and we can see what a phenomenon you are — a virtuoso of this particular mode of perception.

I'd like to discuss the gains and losses of the methodology you have deployed here. Because, in the Joycean model, the real subject is the magma of language. It is neither the characters nor the content, but rather the language that pushes from within itself the language as a living force. Then, there is a danger that, when applied to the session, this model becomes a thing in itself, unrelated to the story of the patient and the analysis. The field is where the narrative or pictorial elements of a relationship are expressed, the elements it is difficult to know where to put. For example, in this case, behind the session lies a question of technique. Just as a reminder: Meltzer, in *The Psychoanalytical Process*,[5] for example, talks about mistakes in technique as the causes of massive projective identification, pains in the belly.

It is as if your way of seeing things entailed the risk of eliminating all memory of the patient's and the analyst's psychic life, so as to focus solely on the language generated in the session itself. You did a pirouette when you talked about the question of the school and the analyst's head. Although the school is mentioned by the patient, this is a reference to the history of the analysis.

So, I think the question I raised, about the risk of doing psychoanalysis without roots, has been fully debated here.

DR FERRO: It is true that the book contains only short vignettes, so I'm glad I've had the opportunity here to look at a whole session with you. I must confess that I cannot always work this way. I need to be happy, cheerful, peaceful, tranquil. Sometimes I am not, and when I am not — which happens frequently — I work with more interpretive models, and try to find opportunities to transform these situations according to these models. I used to have a feeling of guilt in this regard, but now I think they are modes of functioning that must continue to oscillate I do not

5 Meltzer, D. 1967. *The Psychoanalytical Process*. London: Heinemann.

think you can stay with the patient on Row C of the Grid all the time. We have moments of distance, detachment, and in each case we can see what we have gained or lost. It is important to emphasize that the transformations that happen here and now are transformations that then change the patient's inner world and history.

AUDIENCE: We all have a natural tendency to a certain Manichaeism: we see everything we consider good as a narrative derivative of the α function, and everything we consider bad as not being a narrative derivative of the α function. However, when you refer to narrative derivatives of the α function, you are referring to ways of making it possible to think of an emotional experience. In this sense, an attack can also be a narrative derivative of the α function.

I wanted to ask a question relating to this comment: in the work that will be presented during the symposium *Resonances*,[6] you describe the vignette of a session in which the child comes to a scientist, who cuts open an egg and thus prevents the chick from being born. You interpret this as if the child were narrating what you, as an analyst, are doing in the session: preventing something from being born. I wonder if it is not possible to see it the other way round: the child identifies with the scientist who cuts off the interpretation; that is, suppresses it, and thus prevents the birth of a new experience in the session. So, here, in our discussions, we often have the impression that, according to your way of interpreting, the patient is always right and never attacks or destroys a good experience that is built up in the session. I would be grateful if you could express an opinion about this.

DR FERRO: It's not easy … I agree with you when you talk about Manichaeism and the fact that it is essential to shape the possibilities of thinking. It is true that anything, including an attack, may be a narrative derivative of the α element.

I imagine there being a kind of theatre with the patient, where they are a young actor, looking for an old theatre director. There are some very ugly masks in this theatre: the rapist, Jack the Ripper. I don't think you can say to a young actor who steps on to the stage for the first time: "Now, put on the mask of Jack the

6 Ferro, A. 1997. "A sexualidade como genero narrativo, ou dialeto, na sala de análise." In: De A. F. Franca, M.O. (Ed.) 2004. *Bion em São Paulo: Ressonâncias*, São Paulo, Casa Do Psicologo, pp. 175–184.

Ripper". It is necessary rather to show in how many different ways I, as director, can be Jack the Ripper, and how many times I can hurt him, kill him etc. I agree to play the part of Jack the Ripper so that he does not feel this mask as something hideous. Then, at last, he can finally use it; that is, get in touch with his violent and destructive aspects, having seen his director wear them.

I agree with what you said about the child and the egg, except that, for me, this is a later stage, when the patient may regain possession of the problems that are the reason he is there. Obviously, he didn't come to me because I was Jack the Ripper; starting from the first session, I am certain that he is the one who is Jack. My problem is to find a way to make him understand without him becoming terrified and having to defend himself against this possibility.

AUDIENCE: But how does this work with perverse patients?

DR FERRO: Can I say something terrible? It works by taking the good aspects of perversion and trying to understand, within the relationship, how the patient feels things. I remember the supervision of a perverse child who drank urine and had a shoe fetish. He managed to come out of all this when it was possible to show him how he felt humiliated and forced to swallow monstrous things.

What we need to do is to find a way of making sense of perversion within the relationship, but always starting from the point of view of the patient. I don't think we can be very successful if we oppose the patient's point of view. We have to espouse their point of view, render it tolerable and lead it towards our point of view, but only after having looked for it where it is. With a hypochondriac patient, for example, we first have to get to the place where the body is sore, by taking their point of view concretely.

AUDIENCE: In your experience, might this not be regarded as seduction?

AUDIENCE: I think that you would always point to the aspect of suffering, so this would not be seen as seduction.

DR FERRO: Initially, we must grasp the patient's point of view. Then we will have years to change it.

AUDIENCE: The question of perversion brings up the problem of acting-out, but how can we distinguish between acting-out and the narrative derivatives of the $\alpha$ function?

DR FERRO: I would regard acting-out as a kind of acting-in on the part of the analyst. I have patients who have made me do terrible things.

Acting-out regards the patient's ability to evacuate something that is not thought. I believe there is a projective identification of β elements, of non-thought elements. Acting-out is an essentially evacuative mechanism, similar to hallucination. The narrative derivative of the α element, on the other hand, is an image, a record, something that never becomes action or movement.

We must tolerate a certain degree of perversion or manipulation of the setting, always bearing in mind that the perversion of the setting will be narrated again by the patient because the patient's superego is bigger than ours. The patient suffers breaches of the setting more than the analyst. So, if this breach is retold, we have the opportunity to take up the subject again and make a transformation.

ANALYST IN SUPERVISION: At the beginning, while commenting on the session, you said you thought there was a consistent model. I want to know what, in your view, this consistent model is.

Let me add that, in my view, you have shown us very skilfully another light, another impressive model with which to see the session. What I'd like to know is, according to this model, what would you have done with this patient if she had requested another session?

DR FERRO: There is an article of mine about this in the *Porto Alegre Journal of Psychoanalysis*, where I talk about "Claudia and the washing machine".[7] This article talks precisely about this issue of change of session. With that patient, I granted the change of the session and then I paid the price. But I think it is also consistent not to make concessions and to pay the price in any case.

As for the model being coherent, it is a model that takes into account the relationship and the need to interpret what happens in the relationship, making conscious the deepest anxieties of the patient. What's more, it performs the invaluable function of putting the patient in touch with their most horrible fears. It is a model that is not only coherent but also productive; it really helps the patient. It seems that the child feels greatly helped by the analyst. Just think of when she says "Keep going".

7 Ferro, A. 1996. "O diálogo analítico: constuções e transfomações de mundos possíveis." *Rev Psicanal., Porto Alegre,* 3 (1), 47-63.

# Clinical Seminar VII

ANALYST IN SUPERVISION: Paula came to me for an interview in February 1990. I was quite shocked by her size: she was extremely obese, weighing over eighteen stone. She had the face of a teenager, she was dressed in jeans, smock and boots, and she stared straight at me. She is a lawyer, thirty years old, married, and is the mother of a seven-year-old girl. She came to me because she was in love with her boss, a woman, also a lawyer. As she left the interview she asked me: "Do you want me?".

She rarely has sexual relations with her husband, who is partly impotent. She masturbates frequently. She feels attracted to women, although she does not have sex with them, taking pleasure in the fantasy alone. She spent her childhood and adolescence in contact with nature, and often uses animal metaphors and images of plants and trees; things she has a special fondness for.

Her mother was a primary school teacher and has worked all her life to keep a wild husband who is a profligate womanizer. Even now, the couple has a troubled relationship: each constantly threatens to leave the other and they invade their children's lives with their problems. She explains that as a small child she was looked after by her father who, even when she still was only a babe in arms, used to take her to the bar where he gambled and drank. Her father has always been, and continues to be, her big friend, although, from what she says, he's a complete rogue. She is horrified by her mother, who she sees as suffocating and relentless. From childhood on, she was mistreated by her, subjected to seemingly inexplicable punishments that left her confused. The mother is having psychiatric counselling. I received this information about her parents only after two or three years of analysis; previous to that, she did not even remember them.

At the beginning of the analysis, she said that she saw herself as attractive, although she considered other people very different from her: they did not understand her way of talking or way of being. She believes she has special powers that allow her to predict events in daily life. I have frequently witnessed her uncanny ability to register apparently imperceptible details; she is also always in a state of alert towards me.

During the first year of analysis, she would sit on the chair opposite my armchair and would not miss my slightest gesture, showing how she observed everything. She would make comments about how tired I looked, the bags under my eyes, my facial expressions etc. At the end of this initial period, she went to the couch voluntarily, saying: "Look, I don't usually turn my back on anyone, do you see?".

I was very interested in this patient, although, at times, I was almost seized with a sudden panic, the feeling of being attacked.

During the first year of analysis, she talked frequently about incidents of violence, deaths and accidents that had happened to her during her childhood and youth. Then, after a session in which she reported being raped, she pulled out a knife she kept in her boot, explaining that she always carried it with her for self-defence. She asked me to keep it, although she said she would miss it. Later, she finally left it behind completely.

After this period, references to her body and her femininity started to come up in dreams and associations. The clear dissociation between her body and her ego became clear. One day, for example, after I had said to her that she was sheltering emotional experiences within herself, in her body, she got frightened and, pointing to the ceiling, said: "But I'm there", pointing to another place from where she observed everything. Another characteristic of hers was that she reacted, and still reacts, physically to hearing certain words of mine, by moaning, embracing herself or protecting parts of her body, such as her ears. Two months ago, on hearing an interpretation that she found striking, she screamed as if she had been hurt and clasped her chest tightly with great force, making a gesture and saying that she had been shot.

Two years ago, with great embarrassment, she brought with her what she called the first chapter of a text she was writing about her impressions of the analysis and the analyst. This happened at exactly the same time as I was finishing my paper to become a member of the Society, and she was the patient I was describing.

In 1994, she developed panic attacks and depression. She was treated with Paroxetine. Her chronic pain improved and the analysis received a fresh impetus.

Last December, I moved to São Paulo, which caused her great disruption and suffering. At the same time, she left the job she had held for ten years to set up her own firm. She continued the therapy in São Paulo.

Dr Ferro: We can already make a few reflections on what we have heard. What struck me most was the question she asked at the end of the first meeting: "Do you want me?". This suggests that all the previous experiences with her parents meant that she had not been desired. I also thought about the use of metaphors relating to trees and animals, which seem to suggest that she has a very basic, very primitive, relationship with nature and the world. It is as if she had gone through the experience of being invaded by something or someone, as if she had suffered an inversion of parental projective identifications, having to take them while still a child, without having found a sufficiently appropriate terrain where she could offload her fears, anxieties and projective identifications.

I often meet patients who have had early experiences with an unsuitable terrain and have become extremely sensitive to their environment: like a very young child who lived in a forest and, at the same time, had to survive in the face of all the possible hazards, paying the utmost attention to detail, because everything could be dangerous and something terrible might be lurking behind every tree. So, we have the history of this little girl taken along to bars, brothels, which are extremely inhospitable environments for a child. The patient cannot turn her back; she needs to keep her surroundings under control, because turning her back is like turning off the radar.

The moment she begins to trust the analyst and is able to stretch out on the couch is, therefore, extremely important. She not only changes her physical position but also her mental attitude towards the analyst.

Describing these terrible things, she found a place where she could give vent to all the tension, as if, finally, using the terminology of Meltzer, she had met a *toilet-breast* where she could offload her anxieties.

I do not think this is the only possible way of getting a focus on the violence and the rapes, but probably all of the analyst's interventions, however minimal, are perceived as dangerous and violent. Not that the interventions are violent in themselves, but they become so because of her extreme sensitivity. I have already referred to a book by an Austrian author,[1] which tells the story of a child who has the terrible experience of registering every noise in a particularly marked way: if an ant is moving around the remotest corner of the garden, he hears its steps with incredible intensity. This seems to me to be the experience of the patient at the beginning of the analysis, as if she did not have an introjected container that would allow her an idea of internal space. So anything that penetrates the mind is perceived as terribly violent. I believe that, as time passes, she stops feeling she is in a forest and then, when she feels that she is not in a situation of dramatic danger, she can leave the dagger, a moment which seems to coincide with the beginning of the possibility of thinking about her femininity as an internal space capable of containing emotions.

This is a first reading of what we have heard so far, which may or may not be confirmed in the session.

ANALYST IN SUPERVISION: The session took place in October 1996, on a Friday, after an absence of two weeks. She had contracted German measles, and I had not told her that I had been in bed with flu for a week.

ANALYST: Good morning.

PATIENT: Are you ill? What's wrong with you?

ANALYST: Flu.

PATIENT *(lying down)*: Oh ... these viruses are terrible. *(Pause)* I've been very ill for a week. I slept for almost an entire week. I don't know what happened to me, but I feel a huge change in me. I don't know what it is, but I feel that there is something very different about me ... *(Pause)* Wow, you're so hot! *(She fans herself.)*

1 Schneider, R. 1995. *The Brother of Sleep*. New York: Overlook Press.

*I had stopped having a temperature two days before. I had had a high temperature and was still feeling intense waves of heat. At the moment she spoke I was beginning to feel unbearable heat. Other members of my family, who had caught the flu and were convalescing, had had the same symptoms.*

ANALYST: Why do you say this?

PATIENT: Wow! A hot jet is coming in my direction. You're on fire! *(She says this with great conviction.)*

ANALYST: You're right. I don't have a temperature, but I feel these intense waves of heat. It's strange how sensitive you are to what happens to me; that is, to another body, although you often don't feel your own *(because she does not exist)*. You're like a radar, your skin is so porous it lets everything in.

PATIENT: I always feel everything, but I am confused, without knowing if what I feel is mine or someone else's. Now, for example, that didn't happen. I'm feeling your warmth. I realized that it made me feel uncomfortable. I think I feel, for the first time, my temperature; yours is so different and it disturbs me … These days I felt a sensation in my body and it was so nice! I didn't feel I was up in the air, outside myself, but all the time inside myself. *(Pause)* The last few days, I've had huge allergies all over my body, especially in the joints *(she indicates that there are still signs)* and I'm left with an alligator skin. I was happy to see my hard skin. *(She pats the skin on her arm, still dried up, with the other hand.)*

ANALYST: It's good to feel solid. *(Pause)*

PATIENT: The last few days I have been relaxed, letting things happen. My joints were all swollen, I was unrecognizable. I went to several doctors, a cardiologist, a dermatologist, and in the end I went to my general practitioner, who showed me various illnesses in an encyclopaedia. I had the symptoms of various diseases and at that point he gave up … So, I decided to rest in bed.

ANALYST: This time you decided to believe in yourself.

PATIENT: Yes, I just let myself go. You spoke of radar. I think I dreamt about it, maybe it was just a recurrent idea, I don't know. I don't remember. *(Pause)*

My whole skin changed *(shows her arm again)* and I felt as if I were getting stronger. Ah! Now I remember the dream! I was on a submarine and I lowered the periscope and went down to the bottom of the sea and saw wonderful things. I got out of the submarine and I started to swim, without equipment. Just imagine! This week I have felt in this state, inside myself like never before; taking possession of myself. *(Pause)* It may seem funny, but that's how I feel. I am lighter, as if I had sloughed off a skin. Where I come from people say you have to purge yourself, throw everything out. Apparently that's what I did.

ANALYST *(I thought of the fact that when a baby is born, liquid comes out.)*: It seems like a hard birth, where you yourself are the midwife.

PATIENT: I feel like I was born. I'm here *(patting her stomach)*, stronger than ever. You know what? The other day, I went to a bookshop to buy a book on diseases, and I spent the whole afternoon reading the chapter on childbirth. At that moment I didn't understand, but then I thought I might need it one day or other, to help someone. Wow, I never thought of that! *(She is referring to the fact that she has read the chapter on delivery.)*

ANALYST: It's really a big change living inside yourself, feeling embodied, instead of wandering around in space.

PATIENT: I've never talked about the horror of feeling that I'm always wandering around. Today, *(she rubs her hands)* I don't need to look at my hand to know it is there. I feel it is there and that it belongs to me.

*There's a long pause. The session is coming to the end.*

PATIENT: It's cold! How much longer have we got?
ANALYST: Now this cold is yours.
PATIENT: It's mine. *(She stands up, says goodbye and leaves the room.)*

DR FERRO: I just want to say some things that come to mind and then we can go back to the clinical material.

First of all, I am struck by the basic harmony between analyst and patient. The patient has German measles, and precisely at that time the analyst has flu. The analyst writes a paper for the Society and the patient writes the first chapter of her memoirs of the analysis, which suggests a very deep emotional harmony.

This patient has a really great receptive capacity for everything that happens around her, both in relation to the sensoriality and to the emotional quality of the session. It is as if she had thermoreceptors capable of responding to changes in the climate.

This patient has a receptive capacity that works as a thermostat, and allows her to feel the heat coming from the analyst or any other source in the environment.

I also think that "so hot" has something to do with the emotional availability of the analyst. Their talk, from a practical point of view, captures the real waves of heat and, from another perspective, this captures the "warm" availability of the analyst. In fact, in reply to the patient's question, "You're ill, what happened to you?" it does not occur to the analyst to interpret the question or try to understand it. She does the most natural and sensible thing in the world: she answers the question. I'm not saying that you should always answer questions from patients. However, at this moment this patient, with her serious basic deficiencies, needs to feel an absolute receptivity. For her any interpretation of this type of problem would be incomprehensible.

ANALYST IN SUPERVISION: I would like to add something. It is a technical question that keeps troubling me. I have never acted like this with other patients ... I have always asked for supervision, because whenever I tried to give some interpretation or other, she was completely lost, confused, as if I had thrown her out. Some years ago, I started to answer certain direct questions and then I tried to understand why she asked me those things. Otherwise, I would have entered into a state of confusion I didn't understand, and that would have interrupted our contact.

DR FERRO: I do not think that analysis should be totally different from the way we deal with someone at home, in our living room, except at the moment when the rules of the game we're playing become clear. With some patients this happens immediately: they understand at once that there is a setting; they are clear what it means; and they can try to alter it or to attack it (the setting must always be defended tooth and nail). But other patients have no idea and, in these cases, not answering their question would be as if someone came to our house and asked us: "What have you had?" and were given the reply: "Why do you ask?".

During the session an atmosphere of fundamental trust is being created that this patient has never had. Maybe a little idealized, but later the right moment will come to counteract the idealization. There will be a time when it will also be possible to suffer disillusionment. Then there will be a transplant — and here I am thinking of another case I have seen recently[2] — a transplant

2 See Clinical Seminar II.

of roots, which have previously never found any soil and now they find suitable terrain.

This helpful and welcoming atmosphere enables the patient to perform an almost paradoxical operation: it is as if she had an extraordinarily porous skin full of eyes, where every pore was an eye through which she could look at reality and, as she gradually gains trust, each of these pores/eyes could close. This gives her a growing sense of identity and lower permeability to the environment.

The dream is beautiful, with its atmosphere of idealized trust. But for the moment I would not worry about idealization: it is as if the analysis were a submarine world to dive into, to emerge from and to swim in, with no air tank, no dive mask, in an atmosphere of acceptance.

The problems will come later, when the atmosphere of the analysis changes. Of course, there will be moments of disillusionment, anger and frustration, but meanwhile the groundwork has been laid for these transformations to happen in the future. It is as if, at this moment, a basic emotional grammar were being defined, connected to the themes of proximity-separation, warmth-cold, distance-encounter.

First, I would like to hear your views, then we can return to some of the moments in the session in more detail.

ANALYST IN SUPERVISION: I would like to give some information, since the atmosphere of understanding also permeates this meeting. Dr Ferro refers to facts that I have not mentioned here. This woman was a lawyer; she held an important position in an institution that worked with rural workers. When you spoke of lack of roots, I remembered that this patient has spent a lifetime fighting to give land, or a place to these people, and when this started to become known, she changed function and profession.

Another point relates to the pores, the eye. About three years ago, for several months I had a recurrent image of a big eye. In supervision I always drew it with a tail, and gradually it came to resemble a foetus with a large head.

DR FERRO: With a patient like this I would be careful about making an interpretation that, in other circumstances, would be perfectly legitimate: for example, the fantasy of going back to being a foetus and living this kind of almost placental relationship where feelings are always the same. I would not give this interpretation, because I think the patient would take it too much as an accusation and an excessive infantilization.

For the first time, this patient is establishing a basic attunement with someone, and I would not want to disturb this extraordinary fact, always bearing in mind that the problems will come later.

ANALYST IN SUPERVISION: The problems started when I moved to another city.

AUDIENCE: I wanted to ask if you could pinpoint something that occurred *before* the German measles, some interpretation, some movement in your relationship that may have led to this disease.

ANALYST IN SUPERVISION: I can't identify it precisely, but during that year there was a change in the relationship with the female lawyer she was in love with. She no longer idealized her. Currently, they are business partners, both at the same level. She is fighting for her space, but now without the tie that existed before. I feel that this also happened in her relationship with me, as she adapted to the external situation. Sometimes, I make an interpretation, and she tells me: "We've already had this. I don't want to get stuck".

I even realize that she makes new movements, although at other times she returns to the old ones. I would not point to this as something that occurred before the German measles, but as a movement of autonomy, of being inside her own body, of being contained inside her own skin, and being able to tell me: "You can't come in".

DR FERRO: The narrative of the patient can always be regarded as relevant to the analytic relationship. I like the point about land reform in the interests of those who have no land or place. There is also the question of the German measles. I do not think you can ask why the disease has occurred, but rather what is the meaning of the story: "I had the measles". I don't know what the meaning is, but it is generally a disease caught in childhood. And it is as if, finally, she could agree to be a child instead of being left in bars and brothels.

Somehow, I would try to grasp the narrative meaning of German measles without investigating its causes. Viruses exist and I don't think one can attribute to the mind a dominance that explains everything that happens in our body. We can see the narrative meaning of a story, but not the organic cause of what was described, as if it, necessarily, had a psychological correlative.

For this patient it was necessary to find such a situation of attunement, of equality with her analyst-colleague, establishing this enterprise of undertaking analysis with her. With time, there is going to be the problem of the necessary transition from a situation of symmetry to one of asymmetry, equality to inequality. This will be the moment of access to the Oedipal situation. The problems I have predicted refer to this step, when the time is right for it to occur. I would not rush it, because it will happen inevitably.

AUDIENCE: My question concerns the psychosomatic reading of events. I suppose, with regard to fluidity, there was a break in the rhythm of the sessions. Etymologically speaking, rheumatism means blockage of fluids in the joints. I wondered, without neglecting the reading done by the analyst, if perhaps it might be questions of creativity connected to fantasies of the menopause. I endorse the motion that the analysand makes in the direction of the abdomen, and that connects to questions relating to functions of the uterus.

The second question involved in this case relates to how crocodiles are born.

DR FERRO: I am interested to know how crocodiles are born!

AUDIENCE: The eggs are placed outside the body and heated by the father and mother. Crocodiles are a model for us, because certain maternal functions are performed by the father without there being an attack, which in frequent fantasies of us men correspond to the "father womb".

There are subtle things about alligators and crocodiles. A supervisor who studied this subject brought me some photographs showing how the young were put into the mouth and then into the water, without being devoured. The analyst falls into these categories, facilitating the free movement of the analysand. Matters of this nature are "homosexual fantasies".

AUDIENCE: I wanted to add something about the relationship of the crocodile to heat. It seems that a difference of temperature of one or two degrees determines whether the baby crocodile is male or female.

AUDIENCE: I also noticed the psychosomatic symptoms. German measles is an infectious disease that causes damage to the foetus in gestation, such as deafness and other serious disorders. I linked German measles to psychosomatic symptoms and to the crocodile skin, not as something connected to solidity, but as something that enters into the material aggressiveness, which is not addressed.

The basic relation is necessary for this patient, but there is too much sweetness and light.

AUDIENCE: The contributions from other colleagues have made clearer what I was thinking about at the beginning of the session. After an absence of a fortnight, the patient immediately asks the analyst: "You're ill, what's wrong with you?". I was surprised by what she then said to the analyst: "These viruses are terrible". My fantasy, my dream in this context, relates to a patient's fear that events have separated her from the analyst. Both have to be very careful.

DR FERRO: I would like to answer these interesting questions, and point out that I completely agree. Remember that I have always stressed that the problems will come, and they will certainly be numerous.

I think the question of the crocodile is important. With severe patients like this analysand it is essential to allow some gradual development of female crocodiles, in the sense that Bion speaks of the development of the container. Before you put things somewhere, there needs to be a place to put them. At the time, analyst and patient are weaving a large wicker basket, inside which terrible things will take shape.

I would like to remind you of what Bion says about the expansion of the container: it develops by means of a series of emotional threads, woven between analyst and patient, and later on, if the analyst is capable of sufficiently negative capability, the content will take shape like a kind of Big Bang or explosion. Therefore, I have no doubt as to the existence of this problem of aggressiveness, still in the nascent state, which begins to boil in the joints or in these terrible viruses, as the frustration and the anger of this patient must be terrible. Inevitably, this will come out. But the development of the container is fundamental so that the contents will then appear in a non-destructive manner. Certainly, there is also something homosexual, but homosexual in the sense that, for now, container and contained prevail, as if container and contained could not yet co-exist. At this moment, the violence of a primary scene is on another planet. In the session, the homosexual would be represented by the equal functioning of the minds, but it begins to move in a heterosexual direction, as the analyst gradually becomes more receptive to a male and active part of the patient. This is what I was talking about earlier — the problem of the transition from equality to inequality.

AUDIENCE: Several times you have said that the problems will come and that there is no equality. What does it mean to expect that problems arise? From my point of view, from the moment when, in fact, they are not equal, the problems are already present. I am not forgetting that this patient carries a knife and, as someone said, this sweetness may be an artifice. So here is my question: what does it mean to wait for problems to arise? To what extent might another vantage point not allow them to become recognizable?

DR FERRO: I believe that problems need to take shape when both the analyst and the analysis can survive them.

I once had a patient who had a very serious condition, and of whom I was afraid. He was tall and very violent. He talked to me about a violent boxer. Before a fight his opponent's friends would send him a young woman to seduce him and tire him out, hoping that this would help his opponent to win the fight. I had no doubts about this communication, and I was not ashamed of the little bit of seduction that I used towards him to calm him down before I started punching him.

You have understood very well — and are pointing out — all the problems that occur behind this analysis. There are underground problems, of which we perceive small sprouting shoots, but I would not begin to dig up the earth. I would rather wait for the moment when each of these little buds had a chance to grow, and only then would I mention it.

I remember that when that patient told me the story of the boxer, it was the moment I began to understand my fear of him. I perceived the seductive moves I was making to calm him down, so that I could feel relieved and be able to speak with him about all this. But this problem had appeared, brought by the patient himself.

Something must arise somewhere in the field, so that it can be expressed. I have every confidence that the contents will come out, as long as there is a climate conducive to this. I wonder which is better: an analyst with more warmth, who gives birth to female crocodiles, which, at some point, will hand over a dagger; or a colder analyst who gives birth to numerous male crocodiles at an early stage, more than the room can contain, and who perhaps receives some stab wounds. The same reasoning applies to the patient. I do not think that there is a need to punch the patient with early interpretations, because she has already spoken of the rapes and abuse she endured. But I trust that a suitable atmosphere makes it possible for all contents, even the most violent and destructive, to come out and be metabolized. I am in no doubt that an analysis should reach a situation of inequality and conflict and that violence, to be metabolized, needs first to enter the room.

# Clinical Seminar VIII

ANALYST IN SUPERVISION: Michel is nine years old. His parents came to me eight months ago, tormented by the endless questions Michel would ask them every evening while they sat in the TV room, and they couldn't take any more. His mother described it as a ritual, where the questions had little importance in themselves, but were a way of putting off the moment when he had to go to bed.

The family lives in a three-room flat. Michel sleeps with the door open in the room next to his mother. She sleeps in the master bedroom and the father in the TV room, because he snores a lot and the mother cannot sleep when he is next to her in bed. During the holidays, they sleep in two rooms, taking it in turns to sleep with Michel.

Michel is an only child by choice and the mother describes herself as a person who had a difficult "*maternage*" (mothering). She explained that she was very depressed after Michel's birth. She attributes this to the death of her paternal grandmother. As a result, the child's maternal grandmother took care of everything: his grandmother had already been feeding him with a bottle for some time before his mother started to breastfeed him.

Michel is in the third class of the school his maternal aunts and uncles had attended. He was recently transferred there because the parents felt he needed more discipline than he was being given in his previous school. When they came to me, the child had just finished a Jungian therapy that had lasted two and a half years. They thought that it had had no effect.

The father was depressed: he had lost his mother three days before, and his father was in hospital after having a bypass, and did not even know that his wife was dead. The maternal grandmother had had cancer of the colon for months and had had a colostomy.

They had been referred by a mutual friend and the mother had urged me to keep things quiet.

They made no reference to Michel being quite obviously effeminate. He is very big for his age, draws well and seems to feel safe while drawing. He does not use the toy chest. His contact is energized, and his intensity is reflected in his movements. He tests my limits, but calms down when he realizes that I am straightforward with him. He thinks that I should take responsibility for stopping him from becoming anxious. He identifies with the fairy Morgana and the hyena from *The Lion King*.

The mother speaks of Michel's sexual curiosity towards her. She says that it got to the point where he told her he wanted to have a relationship with her, to which she replied that he might feel like that and think about it, but it was not appropriate to talk about it. I have the impression that when the mother brings him to the session, he comes in wiggling his hips a bit more than otherwise. Michel is taking drugs to delay early puberty.

Gradually, as we started meeting, it seemed to me that a feeling of mutual sympathy developed between us. Recently, he has started using the toys from the box.

The session I am going to recount took place in October 1996, and I've given it a title that I'd rather not disclose at the moment.

*When I go to call Michel in, I see that he has come with a man. He's leaning over the reception desk next to his small cousin, who seems to be his miniature. The man says: "Go on, Michel".*

*Still in the corridor, he says: "Everything all right, Marina?". And I say, "Hello, Michel".*

*In the room, I ask who the man is (it's usually his father who brings him). He tells me that it is his maternal grandfather and says he was teaching her the Arabic alphabet. As I saw it was the cousin he was dealing with, I suspected that the child might not really be his cousin but might, in fact, be a girl. Then I say: "Her?".*

PATIENT: Yes, S. *(The girl at the reception.)*
ANALYST: Ah. Then there are things that only you know.
PATIENT: Yes, Marina, there are things that only some people know and not others. That's the way it is.

*He sees that I have brought some carbon paper.*

PATIENT: Oh, to write notes, ha! ha! ha!
ANALYST: What a sadistic laugh: ha! ha! ha!

*He finds my imitation funny and makes what I call a nest on the balcony I have in my room: at one end he puts a chair on the floor and, at the other, another chair on the floor, and between the two he arranges a mattress, making a "U". He suggests we play the same game we played in the previous session, which I shall describe. He sends me a note in "Arabic" — from the Baron Zogaib — and he becomes the postman who comes to deliver it.*

PATIENT: Post! *(Waits for an answer.)*

*I say that I am not as rich as the Baron, that I don't even have paper to write on. (He had put all the paper into his nest.)*

He says: "Oh, put the answer there, on the same piece of paper".

*Then I rip off half of the empty piece of paper and begin to write him a note, again "in Arabic" — but not real Arabic, as neither he nor I know the slightest thing about Arabic.*

*While I reply to the note "in Arabic", he is sitting in what now no longer looks like a nest, but more like a tent, and he is there singing "Arab" music and tearing up a note from the previous session. He scribbles on scraps of paper that become new notes. When I'm finishing writing my note to him, the postman comes along and brings me the pile of notes, saying: "He wants an answer".*

*I send the first note and start writing on the back of each note. The Baron receives my note through the mail and is very pleased to receive a note written "in Arabic". As I write the reply to the notes, he begins to pierce my first note in a manic, agitated, frantic way. This time he no longer spends any time writing. He comes to me and throws the pile of notes in my face, on the table, and says that the Baron wants an answer. I say that it seems he wants to distract my attention by giving me so many notes to reply to. I see him take a piece of paper and draw a heart, but he does not send it to me.*

*While I am replying to the notes, he says he will send me his photo; with fast and accurate strokes he draws a turbaned Sultan (see Figure 7). It's his photo. He hands it to me (he is still the postman), saying it is a photo of the Baron. I say that I will send him my photo.*

*While I draw my picture, he leaves the room saying that he is going to drink some water and comes back holding an empty plastic cup. I hand him my photo and he says, "Wow, Marina, you've taken all this time just to make this drawing?".*

*And I say, "Yes, Michel, not everyone is as brilliant as you at drawing". He comforts me: "Yes, but it came out very well. It looks just like you".*

Figure 7

*He goes back into his tent and brings back the empty glass. He puts the photo I sent him and the love note (the one with the heart) in the glass. From then on the postman disappears. (Since he went out to drink water, the postman no longer appears.) Then he throws the glass at me and I take it, look at what's inside and say: "Hey, he has given me back the photo ... Maybe he didn't like it? Oh, he's sent me a love note".*

*He asks me for the glass and I give it back to him the same way in which he sent it to me, throwing it, with the photos and a love note inside.*

*He takes the note and makes it into a boat by cutting the ends with scissors, all the time humming "in Arabic". Suddenly, he lets out a low, half-hysterical cry, then a loud one.*

*When he lets out this cry, I say: "Goodness, you look like a big man".*

*Then, he lets out a little yelp again. And I say, "That's like a gay cry".*

*He shows me how the cut-out boat has become a shirt and comments that he could cut it another way, but it would be more laborious and that this way it's easier. He says: "No, my name is Baron Michel Farid Zogaib Saad Barbosa da Rosa", and says a lot of other names I don't remember.*

*And I say: "Repeat".*

*He laughs, because he knows he can't repeat it. He says he will write his name. He takes a piece of paper and I say: "This name indicates someone who is really very important".*

*He says there's more to come, that this is only a part. He will write the rest.*

*I say that then it is much more important than it seemed, but we are at the end of the session.*

*He says, "Oh, no".*

*I say, "Yes, Mr Baron must go now".*

*We gather the things together, put them to one side and he throws the cards, the t-shirt and my photo into the rubbish, and I put the photo of the Baron into the chest. By the door, he again emits the same cry as before and I comment: "Look, the gay cry again".*

*Only this time, he looks at me rather worriedly, and asks where that other man is, the big man. Then he shouts loudly.*

*And I say, "Okay, see you next time". (He leaves the room satisfied.)*

DR FERRO: I confess to not being able to follow all the different steps, because I have the text in French. (It's complicated: Italian, French, Portuguese.)

The history of this child is extraordinary. Basically, he has a depressed father and a depressed mother. Of course, he finds himself in a situation of deficient mental hospitality, and probably receives too little primary containment, with the result that he has difficulty getting to sleep, as if he felt a great anxiety about the world that is active during sleep. It is as if he wanted, in every way imaginable, to delay this moment of meeting his phantasms, as if he had never been able to sufficiently internalize a maternal and paternal function, capable of transforming $\beta$ elements constantly into $\alpha$ elements, and transforming the anxieties that form inside him.

What also strikes me is the fact that his precocious puberty is being held up, and that this child, who suffers from such a great shortage of primary care, has had the good fortune to meet this emotionally available analyst.

I've never seen a story of a session with a name like this, which I think is really good. Between the presentation of the material and the beginning of the session, there is a title which is presented as the title of a play, announcing: *The Thousand and One Nights, performed by Baron Michel Farid Zogaib Saad and Marina.*

Even the way in which the session is written is worthy of note. The classic way is to alternate between analyst and patient. Only rarely do we have analyst and patient; elsewhere there is a continuous narrative. I thought it was good that the analyst found this way to offer a poster announcing *One Thousand and One*

*Nights,* and so on, whereby both can be seen as protagonists, which helps us to understand the creation of a field in which the analyst is actively involved in the story that is constructed, without any marked interpretative caesuras. The analyst does not say "the Baron Michel is that part of you that ...", or "some narcissistic part" or "the part that wants to ...", or other similar things. I would say that the analyst puts herself at stake, allowing the real phantasms that were imprisoned there to come out. What comes to mind is Aladdin's lamp, and the genie that comes out when it is rubbed.

This Baron Michel — whose name is a way of saying "there's more to come; wait until I write my full name" — represents the ghosts, the emotions that could not be sufficiently metabolized and have remained trapped inside the lamp, and can now begin to leave, but with a tail because they are so long. It is as if all the phantasms that escape and terrorize the child during the night (when they are not transformed into α elements in dreams), provoking nightmares, anxiety, or at the very least a troubled sleep, as if everything has basically found, in what I would call the transitional space of the session, a sort of Row C of the Grid, where distressing things can be poured out, in order to be thought and transformed.

I found it difficult to follow the entire session, but I liked what I could understand. First of all, there is this "nest" function, and we must bear in mind that the child has not had available parents to function as a nest for him. And then, once he has taken up his position in the nest, the history of Baron Zogaib begins to appear. We do not know exactly what this story means, but I believe that it refers to a fantasy of pampering: a sultan has a whole harem and has plenty of α functions that look after him.

There is a film by Fellini, *8½*, with Marcello Mastroianni, in which the protagonist imagines and, in part, realizes this dream of being a sultan surrounded by lots of women, who, at least as far as I remember, are not there to provide something erotic but rather this total primary attention. Here, the fantasy of the sultan corresponds to this need for the primary nursing he has never had. What I find interesting is that the analyst plays such a major role in the game. It has often been said that a child analyst should simply stay in his place and interpret, but even Melanie Klein played with her child patients; she didn't merely interpret. And here we see an analyst who is not afraid to enter the game, who composes a sonata for four hands.

I would also regard these two aspects, the male and the gay aspects, as two ways in which the phantasms held down under pressure can come out. If we remove the cover completely, the male side comes out, corresponding to the force with which the phantasms emerge. So, I would see "masculinity" as having a very primitive meaning: it is like some pressing content, strong projective identifications that escape in an overbearing and violent way when the lamp is rubbed. Then the gay voice would correspond to the idea of a lid he puts on periodically, which has a very small hole, too small to let these overbearing projective identifications and these pressing proto-emotions pass through. And rather than letting out this male cry (male in the sense of content that presses to be accepted), it only emits this mild, faint sound. His fear of sleep is like an all-covering lid. When there is no cover, the male cry comes out together with the Baron and all his names; and then there is a lid with a small hole, from which this gay cry comes out. It is as if there were some kind of modular system of opening and closing valves through which all these non-digested and non-metabolized facts pass progressively during the session.

The treatment for precocious puberty is something that prevents these undigested facts from getting out; it is almost a way of blocking something that is pressing. By undigested fact, I mean all those situations in this child's history in which his α elements or anguish was unable to find a way of being accepted or worked through, as a result of the minimal presence of his parents. During most of the session, I find that these β elements can be transformed, and what was in danger of being a nightmare begins to turn into a fairy tale. The analyst writes *A Thousand and One Nights,* as if the thousand and one nights of insomnia and nightmares could become the *Thousand and One Nights* of Scheherazade when an α function comes into play.

I think that the story of Baron Michel and Marina is not the only story, but parallel to this, another story begins to take shape which is less "Arabic". In this story, Michel will enter into a direct, emotional relationship with his analyst, not only through the character of the Baron.

We can think of this drawing as representing the movement of a set of β elements to an α element. It is as if there were a set of fragments (all the undigested facts, the β elements, the anxieties that have accumulated and have terrorized the α function of the child, who felt incapable of transforming these elements into α elements, into images) which, thanks to this function — more of a "harem" function than an α function — can be transformed into a representation with a meaning. And this is the Baron, it is Michel himself, and it is an α element; something that can be thought. It would be interesting to make a photocopy, to cut it up into little pieces and then to see if we could compose a figure out of them. According to another model, we would speak of a transition from a state of disintegration to a more integrated and more meaningful situation.

I think the translation from Arabic into Portuguese will be a question of transforming, step by step, these undigested elements into mental images, into α elements, into dreams that are not nightmares.

There are also many technical problems, but now I would like to hear what you have to say.

AUDIENCE: I think there is a character that makes this transition from α elements to β. You spoke very little about the postman.

AUDIENCE: What do you think of this presentation of Michel as such an interesting and powerful person? Is he perhaps covering over his fear that if he does not give the analyst interesting things, she might become like the depressed mother who does not react to his presence?

AUDIENCE: There's one detail I wanted to ask about. Is Michel obese? Does he have breasts?

ANALYST IN SUPERVISION: No, he's just big.

AUDIENCE: It occurred to me to ask this because he is a child who asks questions and the questions are about where babies come from. The parents complain that he asks an infinite number of questions. Question: "Where do I come from?" Since he does not see the parents together, he cannot realize the preconception of being born from parents. I suppose this has created a strange combined parental figure, perhaps a mass or a multitude of people, something monstrous and shapeless, which also has a sadistic quality about it, and which makes it impossible to identify within it a coupling man and woman. Those parents have not made a nest for him. His dream and his desire would be the counterpart of this parental figure; a dream in the sense of a desire, because the Baron represents the desire for idealized identity. He would be a sultan with a harem and I think his physical form, like a huge baby, is a concrete embodiment of this mass.

AUDIENCE: I'm reminded of a film by Joseph Losey, *The Go-Between*. In the film there was a boy who idolized a woman who used him to send messages to her lover. The lover, who likewise sent messages to the woman, also idolized her. And the boy, the son of a waitress, was satisfied with this situation, feeling important and loved by this woman, who belonged to a higher social class. All his life, he entertained the illusion that he was loved by the woman and was fulfilling an important mission. Then, when he is an old man, the woman, older than him, tells him that she had never seen him as a person, just as a messenger.

In the material, the situation is mentioned where his mother is in one room, his father in another and he is in between. My fantasy is that Michel's inability to sleep might have the function of telling stories to the parents, in order not to be confronted with the distressing situation of totally separate parents. The session would be the place where he repeats this with the analyst. The messenger would be an attempt to identify with the father, because he is the sultan, an ultra-powerful father, and at the same time, he transmits this for the analyst to register. Then he abandons the game when he goes to get a glass of water; he is no longer playing the go-between, the postman has disappeared. Finally, it seems to me that instead of being a monstrous combined figure, they are two figures who never meet: the gay, on the one hand, and the big man, on the other. But these two figures never form a synthesis that would enable him to achieve a male identity. I think of this function being suffocated, occupied by the idea of the go-between, of the link between these parents, but he is never able to make internal links, that is, to form his own synthesis.

DR FERRO: Certainly, the postman is important. In the title we have *A Thousand and One Nights*, as performed by the Baron and Marina. The protagonists are not Michel and Marina: Michel at the moment doesn't exist, because he is playing the part of the postman.

This function of the messenger seems important to me. It is almost as if there were a set of undigested facts that need to be metabolized. Then there might be a story between Michel and his analyst. I agree with the idea of the number of phantasms that have accumulated in the mental life of this child. Of course, they are sadistic phantasms who are connected to the idea of rejection, and there are monstrous parental figures etc. I would see the Arab's turban (see Figure 7) as a hydrocephalus, inside which all these undigested phantasms have accumulated, but I do not think you can say all of this to the patient. I believe that progressive alphabetization will gradually diminish the turban, diminish these narcissistic aspects, as all the phantasms that have formed this hydrocephalus will find the opportunity to be metabolized in the relationship with the analyst.

Consequently, for this child, who has a primary deficit with regard to containment, these suffering, monstrous, highly painful aspects must first be stored in the mind of the analyst for a long time. If the analyst were to say: "It is not true that you are a sultan, you are only a child full of desires and anxieties", and emphasized these aspects of need, anguish and terror, this would interrupt the magic of the C Row that we have observed at work. Everything that exists in the hydrocephalus, day after day, must find a way to be metabolized, but almost imperceptibly.

On the other hand, as you know, when a hydrocephalus needs to be alleviated, you should never fully open the valve in the catheter, because there is a risk of immediate death. The valve has to be opened little by little, so as to ease the tension in stages. Gradually, as the child with all his backlog of needs, is emptied (through this catheter-Michel, a messenger of love), the sultan will leave the stage, the hydrocephalic child will leave the stage, and a relationship between the analyst and the child will come to take shape.

There are also more adult aspects to consider, relative to the various problems of identification, the primal scene and the child's sexual identity, where I would think of masculinity in its very archaic form, like the tension of the liquid that compresses and presses inside the hydrocephalus. For this reason, I thought the question about obesity and breasts was important.

AUDIENCE: I would like you to speak more about the question of revitalization, interpretation, the alphabetization of these phantasms.

AUDIENCE: To what extent should the child's problems be attributed to the lack of primary care by the parents, and to what extent is there something innate in him that makes him blind to these attentions? That is, to what extent is there a real lack of containment on the part of the parents, and to what extent is there something innate in the child that transforms something the parents might have given into absence?

AUDIENCE: I was curious to know if Arabic has any relevance in the family history of Michel.

ANALYST IN SUPERVISION: Both the mother and the father are of Arabic descent.

DR FERRO: It is worth pointing out that the question of interpretation is not decisive. Perhaps this is not the best way to express this, and we need to expand the concept of interpretation. If by interpretation we mean rigid transformation ("You behave like this with me because ...") that would serve no purpose. If we expanded the semantic scope of the term interpretation to include all the changes that the analyst makes in the session, especially the narrative changes, then we could say that the analyst's activity works only through interpretations. Thus, it is necessary to establish what we mean by interpretation, in the sense that classical interpretations need first to find a locus where they can be placed.

In the case of a hydrocephalus, I cannot put anything inside it; if there is a container that cannot hold any more, I cannot put anything inside it, but I need to make some interventions — which, from my point of view, are interpretations — to promote the progressive alleviation of the hydrocephalus. This is where the creativity of the analyst comes into play: they need to find a way to say things without upping the voltage. We have here an example of how narration can make this character come onto the scene and then, step by step, we can observe the future evolution of the Baron and the other protagonists.

The first time I made an interpretation that I termed "narrative" was with a patient who was terrifying, extremely aggressive and violent, who never approved of anything I said. If I spoke of his aggression or his anger, he mocked me; if I said that he was afraid of my aggression and my anger, he said I was talking nonsense. There was no way of speaking about this climate of fear and violence that I started thinking about two hours before he arrived. Then one day, not knowing what else to do in the session, I said: "With you I feel like I am in one of those movie scenes in the Wild West, when a glass falls and everybody in the saloon pulls out a gun and starts shooting". He made a huge smile and from there on we started talking through westerns, and went along this road for some time. It was the way we discovered to communicate what was happening in the analysis, using the narrative elements of the C Row. I see it as an interpretation when I say: "I feel like I am in a western". And it is very different from saying: "Inside you there is a destructive part, etc....".

As for the last question, I do not think we should think of one of the two poles of the relationship, but rather of the way that type of relationship works. In this situation, we have a story told by the parents, where the problem is clearly a major maternal and a major paternal depression. So something did not work owing to the parents' failure to provide a mental environment, which as we have seen was "reactivated" by the constant stream of questions.

We can make sense of the harem aspect in two different ways: as something very narcissistic; or as an expression of Michel's dream of a great surgical team. For this reason, narcissism always has another aspect that hides very early wounds, very primary needs, and I think this is a particular way of looking at narcissism. Yesterday evening; we discussed this,[1] and I repeat it here because maybe someone was not present. I described a child with a serious narcissistic disorder who considered himself a thousand times more intelligent than Leonardo da Vinci; a genius, a mathematician, a musician (and, in fact, he really was good). One day, he drew a diamond, saying that if this diamond were put in a bowl containing a special liquid, we would see that it was not a diamond, but rather a very fragile crystal.

This special liquid in the bowl has to be the gaze of the analyst, capable of not getting annoyed, not competing with the patient's narcissism, but always able to see the hydrocephalus beneath the disorder, and the suffering and the need beneath the narcissism.

The "Arab" question implies the need to reconstruct an old story, and to be able to metabolize everything that had previously been meaningless.

1 See Thematic Seminar II